Praise

'Any finance professional embarking on a career in a high-growth business will benefit from reading *Financial Leadership Fundamentals*. Alysha Randall shares personal lessons emphasising the importance of a growth mindset, learning how to add strategic value and developing leadership skills applicable to finance careers. It's an accessible read for any busy executive full of practical tips. This book will become a formative text for all CFOs of the future.'

— **Guy Hutchinson**, tech CFO and Co-founder, Startup CFO Community

'In *Financial Leadership Fundamentals* Alysha encapsulates both the magic and the harsh realities of being a CFO in the startup world. Covering the breadth of the role, from managing tough relationships to the technical skills of financial reporting and audits. This is the handbook every CFO or aspiring CFO needs in their bag.'

— **Jennifer Pearson**, Founder, Treasury Edge

'This book is a toolkit for being an effective CFO in a startup and scaleup. Drawing on her experiences from startup, scaleup CFO and fractional CFO roles, Alysha provides hugely valuable guidance on how to grow towards the CFO level. She provides direct examples and an honest presentation of the CFO role, including the less glamorous aspects. My favourite part: the action lists at the end of each chapter, which allow you to check where you are and refresh your learning quickly. As an experienced CFO in corporate, scaleup and startup environments, I would have loved to have had this practical framework to facilitate my journey.'

— **Natacha Robert**, Director and Fractional CFO, Evergreen Consulting

'*Financial Leadership Fundamentals* is awesome! I love this book and I can't wait to shout about it. The information in here is brilliant, and I genuinely wish I'd had this advice when I was at GoCardless. I love the case studies included as well.'

— **Corinne Thompson**, Founder and CEO, Ecap Financial

Financial Leadership Fundamentals

How to become a CFO in a startup or scaleup

Alysha Randall

Rethink

First published in Great Britain in 2025
by Rethink Press (www.rethinkpress.com)

This book is dedicated to my wonderful and supportive family, David, Lily and James, and my loving parents, Trudi and Neville.

Contents

Foreword

I first met Alysha in a Lebanese restaurant in North Acton in 2006. She was interviewing to be UK financial controller of LoveFilm (the distant predecessor of Amazon Prime Video), and we did the interview in the kebab shop because it was an extension of our overflowing office. That meeting epitomises what working in an early-stage business can be like. I have worked, mostly as CFO, in eight startup or scaleup companies, except of course for Dell and Amazon, which might be seen as exceptions. I still count them as scaleups, even though they were multibillion-pound companies at the time, as they were founder-led, still growing like crazy, chaotic at times and constantly looking for how to reinvent themselves as they grew ever bigger. Working as a CFO in an early-stage business, whether a startup or scaleup, can provide both an incredible challenge and also excellent experience. Mostly it is also a lot of fun!

In *Financial Leadership Fundamentals,* Alysha highlights many of the challenges that you can face as a startup or scaleup CFO and provides practical guidance on how to overcome them. There are two challenges that stand out for me. Firstly, as a CFO you can often be part of a small team (and sometimes you are the team), so you will need to be ready to cover significant breadth – possibly from fundraising through to posting invoices; as well as areas outside of your functional expertise – often legal and HR. You may, though, also be expected to deal with IT, facilities management and anything else that can help keep the company moving forward. Secondly, if the business is successful, you will need to reinvent the finance function on a regular basis, constantly looking ahead to see if it will be fit for purpose in six months, a year and two years' time. If this sounds like the sort of challenge that you would relish, then this book is for you.

This is also why early-stage businesses provide an environment in which you can gain unrivalled experience. You might join a company when you are the only finance person or where you have just a small team. If the journey is successful, though, and you go all the way through to exit for the initial shareholders or for an IPO (initial public offering), you'll learn many of the skills needed to be a CFO. Early-stage companies don't always need or can't always afford an experienced CFO, so they may initially draw on the experience of an adviser, board members or investors in managing their financial strategy and hire someone less experienced to be more of a head of finance or financial controller. However, if you are lucky enough to be that person, you can get an amazing ride, and provided you focus on your own personal development and grow with the role, you can come out at the end with an amazing set of experiences.

Don't expect a fancy corporate world with lots of support functions to guide you on your journey. However, in this book, Alysha has used her experience and expertise to lay out a path for you through what might at first seem like an impenetrable maze. If you enjoy adventure and you are a self-starter who is excited about embarking into new and unknown territory, you will have a lot of fun and get a lot of satisfaction from your work.

Since that first meeting in 2006, I've enjoyed observing Alysha grow as a business leader, first at LoveFilm and then at Funding Circle, then supporting a myriad of founders at many different startups, and now helping others go on the journey that she has successfully taken. I am sure you will benefit from reading her thoughts, advice and experience.

Jim Buckle
C-level executive and NED; CFO, Gousto

Introduction

Are you drowning in tasks in your current finance role and feeling the weight of proving your worth as a great leader to the founder / CEO?

Have you recently stepped into the chaos of the startup and scaleup world, now discovering that your previous conventional finance training isn't suitable for this kind of environment?

Are you an established player in this startup industry, yet that next step – claiming the leadership role you know you're ready for – seems just out of reach due to a lack of confidence or direction?

Are you wondering how you can get that CFO or finance director role in a startup or scaleup?

I get it. I've been there.

I've been working with startups and scaleups as a finance leader since 2006, and I have seen and learned a lot. I started in this industry for a startup, LoveFilm, which was eventually acquired by Amazon. I worked on the transition, flying often to Seattle and seeing firsthand what a startup can become. I then moved on to preparing a scaleup, Funding Circle, for an IPO. Both businesses were fast moving, and I had to learn quickly to keep my head above water.

As I love that early-stage frenzy of startup life, I created my own company, Fast Growth Consulting, and have worked for many founders and startups since. I've had the luxury of professionalising the finance function of many companies such as VenueScanner, Collagerie, Just Move In, Legl, SideQuest VR and Super Payments in the UK and US, and TR8 in Singapore. I enjoy seeing how much a finance function can change within just a few months.

I enjoy training new and aspiring finance directors and CFOs so have created online courses and group training sessions to help a bigger audience. Using my courses I have trained new and aspiring finance directors who want not only to take ownership of their leadership role, but also to understand what the role entails. I've also been an expert facilitator for FourthRev finance courses. I have been interviewed on several podcasts, including *CFO 4.0* and *CFO*

Insights, and I have been featured on websites such as those of LegalEdge, CFO Connect and The Female Lead. I have some amazing stories to tell and look forward to sharing them with you in this book. I am also writing to you from personal experience.

I clearly remember learning the hard way in my first leadership role. Not only did I misunderstand what was expected of me and lack the confidence to speak up in meetings, but I was also working so hard that my social life and relationships were suffering. My director gave me some strong, negative feedback, which highlighted the strain I was under. I knew I had to act quickly, or I was going to be out of a job. I spent a year reading everything I could, meeting every CFO I knew, and enrolled in a Women In Leadership course at Oxford Business School.

Thankfully, I managed to turn everything around and received praise in my next annual review. I don't want this to happen to you. This is the book I wish I had back then.

The startup and scaleup world is a hectic business. Everything moves fast, and anything can change overnight. What may have worked for you one week is completely out of date the next. It can be hard to keep up. You may also be the only finance person in the company or, if you're lucky, have one or two others in your team. The founders, leadership team and board of directors turn to you, seeking insights and information that they hardly communicate or have difficulty articulating, silently expecting you to decipher their unspoken needs. Amidst the frenzy, the founder lives and breathes their business, trying to keep their head above water, leaving little time for guidance or mentorship to help you in your leadership role.

Your startup may not even have an HR department, let alone a learning and development (L&D) department. Here the finance leader often becomes the de facto HR department, but where do *you* turn for support in this relentless environment? How are you going to get the guidance and mentorship you need as a new or aspiring leader?

Unlike the structured learning and mentorship programmes in large corporations or accounting firms, where accountants are supported in their career growth, the startup ecosystem offers no such avenues. You might feel isolated, firefighting day after day, struggling to prove your worth and questioning whether you're destined to remain in management limbo. Are you going to be overshadowed as the founder hires above you instead of promoting you? Even worse, are you nervous you'll be asked to leave the business and then struggle to find a new role, only to have to start the cycle all over again?

I'm here to tell you there's a different narrative awaiting you. The startup and scaleup world can be challenging, but there is a way to navigate your way through the noise and the chaos. In *Financial Leadership Fundamentals,* I'll guide you through the roadmap of evolving into an exceptional finance leader for a startup or scaleup. You'll learn to use your existing strategic abilities and show your value to the founders, leaders and board members.

Achieving a leadership role doesn't mean you need to sacrifice your life to work. You can find balance between a successful career, your mental health and life. There will be some tough days, but with guidance you can regain your work–life balance and not feel like you're spiralling into burnout.

My structured framework, suggested techniques and ideas can lead to you becoming a strong finance leader. *Financial Leadership Fundamentals* lays out a clear blueprint for bringing your leadership skills to the forefront, and it includes actionable steps so you know what to do in your role.

By the time you have finished reading this book, you will have:

- A better understanding of the culture of startups and scaleups and the nuances of this industry
- Step-by-step actions that you can implement immediately
- The confidence to step into that leadership role and own it

This book is divided into five parts, with each part covering a step in our Financial Leadership Fundamentals Framework, illustrated below. This framework has been built based on my many years of experience of working with founders and finance leaders. I now use this framework for every client and for all my students.

	Leadership and mindset	✔ Confidence to be part of the conversation in the board room ✔ Have the right balance of emotional intelligence ✔ Develop strong relationships with all stakeholders
	Keeping the lights on	✔ Ensure that all financial statements are accurate ✔ The company meets all compliance requirements ✔ Understanding of current cashflow and cash burn
	Monitoring and reporting	✔ Strong, regular and consistent reporting ✔ Constant review reporting to ensure they're accurate ✔ Review, improve and automate all processes
	Adding value	✔ Prepare for any fundraise, be it equity or debt ✔ Constant review of metrics, KPIs and trend analysis ✔ Growth models, budgeting, scenario testing
	Strategy	✔ Team developments long term ✔ Business and product growth, competitive advantages ✔ Margin improvements and profitability enhancements

The Financial Leadership Fundamentals Framework

The framework provides the stepping stones, delivering an understanding of what it means to be in a leadership role:

1. **Leadership and mindset:** How a strong mindset will allow you to confidently step up to the top job
2. **Keeping the lights on:** The practical side of day-to-day financial management
3. **Monitoring and reporting:** Another practical step, completing the non-negotiable baseline of a solid and trustworthy finance department
4. **Adding value:** Including fundraising – a vital part of startups' and scaleups' existence
5. **Strategy:** How the finance leader can work with the founder and the rest of the leadership team to support the business's strategy and direction

If you follow this framework, implementing the actions I outline in this book as well as downloading the templates and resources I share, you will gain breathing space and confidence, and that leadership role you are in or aiming for will soon be safely in your hands.

Note: You'll find a glossary of terms at the end, which you may need to refer to as you read this book.

To access the book resources mentioned throughout the book, go to www.financialleadershipfoundations.com/bookresources or scan this QR code:

PART ONE
LEADERSHIP AND MINDSET

This is the first part of the Financial Leadership Fundamentals Framework. The jump from a manager role to a leader position is huge. It largely has to do with how you think about yourself, how you think about the business, and what you contribute. Before I discuss the practicalities of the role, let's talk about what it means to be a leader.

1
What Is Leadership?

There are reams of literature on what leadership is, and you have no doubt seen this topic everywhere, including on social media. I completed a leadership course specialising on the theory of leadership and leadership skills. That, combined with years of experience, led me to the conclusion that a key factor is how you think, behave and feel like a leader, rather than like a manager.

My thoughts on leadership

A great place to start this chapter is considering the words of Indra Nooyi, former CEO of PepsiCo. She explains that it is difficult to define leadership and even harder to define good leadership, but that getting people to follow you to the ends of the earth proves that you are a great leader (Rani, 2024).

While there are many different leadership models, methods, means and styles, the end goal is for people to follow you towards your vision and mission. No matter how you do it – whether you approach leadership in a passive way or a more extreme or aggressive way – the end goal is the same.

I remember my first leadership role clearly. I had just progressed from reporting in to a CFO. I was now reporting directly to the founder and CEO and was assigned a small finance team. The company I was working for was growing at a rapid pace, and the four of us were working ridiculous hours.

Looking back, I can see clearly that I had not fully embraced that leadership role. I had no vision or mission or long-term goals. I certainly wasn't confident in my role, and I was only trying to keep my head above water. I went to leadership team meetings and hardly contributed unless the topic was on the monthly results. My team was loyal to me as I was working harder than they were, and I was always kind to them, but they weren't going to stick around forever. I wasn't teaching them more than the tasks at hand, and promotions were out of the question because I wasn't thinking about building a proper finance function.

I was in over my head, and burnout was on the cards.

If I had fully understood leadership and tried to implement longer-term solutions and goals, over time a more structured and strategic approach would have saved the team lots of time and stress. Especially stress.

When thinking about leadership in general, not just from a finance perspective, there are three key parts of a leadership role:

1. Communication
2. Strategy
3. Development

1. Communication

Communication is critical, and leaders spend a lot of time communicating. Prior to the Covid pandemic, a lot of communication was verbal: in meetings, standing up at all-hands meetings, and talking with third parties and with the board. Now that more people are working remotely, written communication is just as important as verbal communication, and sometimes even more so.

2. Strategy

Thinking strategically – essentially, thinking longer-term – is the second key part of leadership. Working with fast-growth businesses, it's easy to focus purely on what's happening right now: *Oh, my goodness, there are six fires that I need to put out. How am I going to hit tomorrow's reporting deadline?* Your day-to-day thinking can be short-term, particularly if you're in a financial management control role where you don't need to think much further than a month out.

With a leadership finance role, month end is important, but longer-term is also key. Within startups and scaleups things change quickly, so identifying growth opportunities, reducing potential risks and reviewing longer-term plans are big parts of any leadership role.

3. Development

To start with, you want to think about how you can develop your team. For example, if you have unqualified accountants working for you, and you're mentoring them in becoming qualified accountants, you can help them work towards a controlling role or financial planning and analysis (FP&A) role.

You also need to focus on self-development. It's much harder when you're a qualified accountant to find time for self-study and to learn about changes in the industry and improving your role. A good start is reading this book! Self-development is on your radar, and it's incredibly important that you continue to study and learn.

The difference between management and leadership

Earlier in my career, as an inexperienced finance leader, I didn't understand the difference between management and leadership. I honestly thought a leader was someone who kept their department's tasks in order and was part of boardroom discussions. In doing just that, I was behaving as a brilliant manager, but my approach wasn't strategic at all. I wasn't acting as a leader.

It's easier to explain what leadership is by comparing it with management. Management is the optimal way to accomplish tasks and achieve goals. Leadership is the art of motivating a group of people to act towards achieving a common goal. Management is much more operational, and leadership is much more visionary. To quote Andy Dunn, CEO of Bonobos: 'Leadership is inspiring people. Management is keeping the trains running on time' (Dunn, 2017).

There are clear differences between the job descriptions for a finance manager or a financial controller and that of a finance director. For a finance manager or controller, tasks include monitoring and analysing the data, producing reports, managing debtors and creditors, managing cashflow, calculating taxes, managing staff expenses and overseeing daily operations. All these tasks are specific. You come in every day knowing what to expect.

With a leadership role – director or CFO, for example – typical elements of the job description are playing a key role in the formulation of strategy, providing support and insight to the board, making critical business decisions, raising finance, establishing KPIs for the teams, creating visibility trends, building and managing a finance function, leading a team, and ensuring the controls are appropriate for scaling a business. They're very forward-looking functions.

Particularly in finance, managers own the transactions, while leaders own the transformation. The role of a financial controller or finance manager includes understanding and taking responsibility for all the transactions. The leader, meanwhile, will be fully involved in the controlling side of the business. Examples of this work include changing processes, addressing issues, reviewing the way the profit and loss statement (P&L) looks and changing the structure of the reporting in preparation for a fundraise. The leader reviews the transactions and reporting holistically, whereas managers dig down deep into the details.

As a side note: in a smaller business a finance director will often need to act as a manager as well as a leader because there may not be a finance manager or controller.

Steve Jobs has been quoted as saying that management is about persuading people to do things they do not want to do, whereas leadership is about inspiring people to do things they never thought they could do.

In general, managers are reactive, and leaders need to be proactive, though a considerable portion of the leadership role can be ambiguous. A perfect example of this is when I worked as a finance director at Funding Circle. The financial controllers reporting in to me were very reactive, thinking about management accounts, reporting on what had already happened, always looking backwards. If a problem arose, they dealt with it at that stage. I also had responsibility for the FP&A team, who thought about the future. They were always budgeting and forecasting and looking forwards.

When I was managing those two teams, once the financial control team had become a well-oiled machine, churning everything out every month, I spent most of my time working with the leadership team and my FP&A team. As a finance director, I was looking forward most of the time but also looking back to make sure everything was accurate. Even more important was what the backward-looking data was telling us about the future. Was the business heading in the right direction? Would it meet its goals? Or did it need to make some changes?

In my opinion and experience, the transition from management to a leadership role is much bigger than the jump from an unqualified to a qualified accountant. This is largely due to there being no set programme to follow in becoming a leader, while

CIMA/CPA/ACCA/ICA come with a required mentorship framework. It's therefore important to understand what leadership is to help with that transition.

The different types of leadership

I had a chance to explore six leadership styles while studying at Oxford's Saïd Business School, which I will discuss here. It's helpful to understand some of the different styles and when they are useful for certain situations. You may find that you naturally gravitate towards one or two of the leadership styles. Particularly in a crisis, it is also worth looking at the different options and seeing how they can best work for you. The six leadership styles are as follows:

1. Visionary
2. Commanding
3. Pacesetting
4. Coaching
5. Democratic
6. Affiliative

1. Visionary

Ultimately, this style of role focuses on sharing the company's vision, thinking about goals and, at a high level, mapping out how to get to that vision and those goals. Next you leave the team to get on with the process as they know what they're working towards.

This style is best when leading a team or a whole company, as it can help a company get through a lot of change. Sometimes it can be also used at a time of crisis.

The negative side of this style is that it can ignore short-term priorities and set unrealistic goals, so it can be patronising, particularly when you are leading a team of experts.

2. Commanding

This is a military style of working – very much *Do as I say*. It is useful when there is a crisis, when you adopt the style on a short-term basis. It is also used when you need to set high performance standards and can lead by example, and when you need to demand a lot from your team.

This leadership style is often seen to be used long term in competitive environments such as in investment banks, and it can encourage quick wins and high performance. Ideally, though, it's probably best to be used only in the short term in less competitive situations.

Problems with this kind of leadership revolve around culture and retaining a team. Highly competitive and stressful environments make it difficult for people to maintain this pace of work for long periods of time.

3. Pacesetting

With this leadership style the leader creates the pace for achieving goals, particularly short-term goals. As the name suggests, it drives the team forward to achieve the set goals.

Like Commanding style, Pacesetting is suitable when standards need to be improved over a short amount of time and to hit short-term goals.

Pacesetting style does create a competitive environment, which can be detrimental in the longer term. It also requires a task-based environment and doesn't allow for a high level of communication and feedback to the team. A pacesetting leader is focused on getting tasks done, with little time for hand-holding or addressing mistakes.

4. Coaching

As the name implies, this style focuses on developing the team's abilities and building the team's strengths. The leader is empathetic and works closely with their colleagues in nurturing the team.

In the longer term, this leadership style can build great morale, encouraging retention and loyalty.

The challenge with this style is that not all team members necessarily want to be coached. Coaching-style leadership also assumes that the leader's skills are relevant to and required by the team they're trying to coach.

5. Democratic

Democratic leadership style encourages collaboration within the team. The leader gets input from the team, and the team and leader work together on problems and solutions.

Like Coaching, this method is great for longer-term retention, culture and morale.

The challenge with this method is that it can take longer for decisions to be made and hitting short-term goals may be difficult. It therefore isn't a particularly useful style during a crisis.

6. Affiliative

This style revolves around developing emotional bonds with the team. It's almost about becoming friends with your team members.

Affiliative style works well when you want to develop trust and loyalty. It boosts culture, and the team members feel they're really part of the team.

The challenges with this style are the potential for poor performance, both at an individual level and for the team. An individual may not upskill in their role and the team may not hit the goals they ideally should for the business to drive forward.

Looking at these six leadership styles, it's important to highlight that you need to aim to be your authentic self. Work out which two suit you best, for the longer term and for short-term crises and challenges.

Leading a finance function

Throughout this book, we will be going through many specific leadership skills, tasks and mindsets. First, though, I want to introduce you to three high-level leadership skills, which you can implement almost immediately:

1. Planning
2. Performance
3. Problem management

1. Planning

A great example of planning is thinking about how the finance function should look in the future, when the company is bigger than it is today. As a leader, you should be planning how the finance function should look in twelve months' time, or even further in the future. You're not just hiring people to fix problems; you need to develop a well-thought-out department.

Measuring this against business size is useful. Different factors – such as transaction requirements, reporting, a statutory audit or the business needing to be regulated – will come into play and will require a bigger team to manage them.

Similarly, processes will need to be carefully planned. If the company was three times the size, would your processes today manage that volume? Often, especially with small businesses, the answer is no.

CASE STUDY: Thinking ahead

I remember working for a regulated business where the required reconciliations were performed manually every single day.

As the company grew, so did the number of transactions, to the point where we needed to hire another person to manage the data and ensure that the business was compliant.

Eventually, these processes were improved and implemented to deal with the growth of the business. However, if this had been done earlier, we would have avoided the tougher challenges of implementing the changes under increased time pressure and workloads.

When you're in a leadership role, you can't think only about your own department – you have to think about the whole business. When presenting the operational strategy and products to your customers, always have this question at the back of your mind: *Would the business be able to handle this if it was three times the size it is now?* Ask yourself: *Can the finance team deal with a business three times the size using the resources that we have today?* Then make sure you challenge the business on the answers to those questions.

2. Performance

When working as a junior or mid-level accountant, you're judged on how hard you work and how much you know. If you make every effort and get through all the tasks that need to be done, you'll be brilliant at your job. When you're a leader, though, that's no longer what matters – performance is about what is delivered. It's the output that matters.

If you're in work every day of the week from 7.30am to 10pm, if your output isn't where it should be, that's how you're going to be judged. Your performance will be judged not only on hitting those deadlines but also on whether you are adding commercial value to the business.

For example, I worked with a finance leader who would always miss deadlines but would always have a reason for that not being their fault. *The general ledger software was down for a day, We didn't get the KPIs in time, The C-suite were at an offsite and didn't give us their expenses,* etc. Unfortunately, from a leader these excuses aren't good enough. Planned mitigation, allowances for issues and longer-term deadline date movements are under the leader's remit. Don't miss deadlines. Leaders will be judged on making sure that all output that comes from them and their department, and their core team, is up to scratch.

3. Problem management

Leaders ideally need to ensure that the small issues are dealt with before they become big problems. In finance a perfect example is the balance sheet, wherein reconciliations sent by the team are reviewed regularly – at least quarterly – and in detail, to eliminate potential future issues on the P&L.

This is also important when mitigating against risk and preventing fraud. Ensuring there are processes and policies in place to mitigate against any internal or external fraud is a big part of a leader's role. When something goes wrong, the first question will always be, *How did it happen?*

Summary

In this chapter we have looked at what leadership is, the difference between leadership and management, the different leadership styles, and initial thoughts on being a finance leader.

Actions for you:

- Look at the responsibilities and tasks you currently have within your role. Classify them, specifying which are management or leadership duties.
- Look at the different leadership styles covered in this chapter and work out which two resonate with you. Ensure at least one works well within a short-term crisis and one works well in the longer term.
- Reserve time in your calendar for planning. Schedule a monthly recurring meeting that you always adhere to.
- Ensure you understand what your deadlines are and work out how to stick to them.
- Make a note of potential issues that are currently ignored or overlooked within your team and your company – and fix them now.

2
Developing A Leadership Mindset

In leadership roles the right mindset is just as important as the right practical skills. With the right mindset will you be a better leader, and you will enjoy the role more. In this chapter we'll discuss how you can ensure your mindset is ready for your leadership role. I'll also cover the topics imposter syndrome, speaking up in meetings, and asking dumb questions (or rather, that there is no such thing as a dumb question).

Confidence leads to leadership, not the other way around

Before I became a leader, I made the mistake of thinking that when you get that FD or CFO leadership role, you automatically become confident because you've got a fancy new title. However, speaking from experience, the confidence doesn't just appear. It is something you need to work on yourself.

Somebody must have believed in me to give me that role. Maybe they thought they'd give me a chance, or they saw something in me that perhaps I don't see.

My confidence was very low early in my finance leadership career. I would sit in leadership team meetings with twenty other people in the room. Lots of conversation was happening, but unless people spoke to me specifically about finance elements, or I was presenting the monthly results, I pretty much stayed silent. I never voiced my opinion, I never gave my thoughts, I never raised a concern. I sat there watching everyone else, thinking I didn't have anything useful to contribute.

Because my confidence was so low, I also didn't flourish in my leadership role. As a leader, you *need* to be able to contribute. Finance has access to so much data and resources that the business needs to hear from the finance leader. It was something I really had to work on.

Now, when I'm training new and aspiring CFOs within startups, we tackle leadership and mindset before getting into other elements of the role. If you want to be a good leader, you need to have the confidence to add value to the business, to share your ideas, to give insight – all the things a CFO is expected to do. This isn't only about getting over the fear of presenting – it is more about confidence within yourself. Whether or not you've already got that CFO role, you need to work now on your self-confidence.

Methods I have personally used to help improve my confidence include:

- **Taking stock of good feedback:** I have a folder in my inbox called 'Good feedback', where I file exactly that – any good feedback I've received. We are wired to remember the negative and constructive feedback, and we sometimes need to be reminded that we have skills and are good at our job. File any good feedback for those days when you need a confidence boost and a reminder of your strengths.
- **Reflecting on experience and goals achieved:** It's always worthwhile to look back and see how much you have learned throughout your career and the things you have accomplished.
- **Keeping an eye on self-talk:** As a starting point, notice when you put yourself down and talk negatively to yourself. That won't help your confidence levels. Recognising when you do this is a good start, and then reversing this self-talk will work wonders.
- **Realising it's OK to make a mistake:** Even the best leaders in the world make mistakes, so don't

be afraid of them. Instead, view each one as a lesson – learning from a mistake can be more valuable than never making one.

If you have a growth mindset (meaning you believe you can grow your own abilities through dedication and hard work), as opposed to a fixed mindset (believing your abilities are set in stone), anything is possible. A growth mindset means you can learn from your mistakes, which you don't mind making, and you don't have to constantly prove that you are good enough at your role.

In her brilliant book, *Mindset,* which I recommend you read, Dr Carol S Dweck explains, 'Even in the growth mindset, failure can be a painful experience, but it doesn't define you. It's a problem to be faced, dealt with, and learned from' (Dweck, 2012). She goes on to explain how people with a fixed mindset can translate a failure to their identity, making them feel *they* are a failure rather than only that they have failed at one thing. Dweck highlights that, when recruiting astronauts, NASA specifically sought out people with growth mindsets. They rejected applications from people who had not experienced significant failures in life, instead selecting applicants who had moved on positively from challenging experiences.

There are many books that can help you with your mindset. You can access a long list of books

I recommend by visiting www.financialleadership-foundations.com/bookresources.

Dealing with imposter syndrome

According to the British Medical Association, people who experience imposter syndrome feel inadequate, despite their evident success (Home, 2024). Chronic self-doubt can make people feel threatened, isolated and fraudulent, which can eventually lead to burnout.

Imposter syndrome has been talked about a lot over the last decade. In a British YouGov survey in 2022, 66% surveyed say they suffered from some form of imposter syndrome (Kirk, 2022). In 2020 a USA KPMG study that found that 75% of all women executives have suffered from imposter syndrome during their careers (KPMG, 2022), so this is far from uncommon. While men also suffer from imposter syndrome, it is more prevalent amongst women.

I don't know many senior leaders who haven't at some stage in their career suffered from some form of imposter syndrome. I have certainly suffered from it, particularly when I first became a finance director. I can still feel slightly like an imposter, especially when meeting someone who is impressive. I then find myself negative self-talking, which I must rectify.

How to know if you suffer from imposter syndrome

If you achieve some level of success, or you receive a promotion and you're not able to take ownership of the success, you may feel like a fraud in your role or in a meeting, and you'll likely feel you're scared of being found out. You will probably think that any personal accomplishments are due to someone else's help rather than you having earned them.

Having a lot of self-doubt, negative self-talk or being a perfectionist can hinder you. You may find it difficult to take pride in anything that you have accomplished. These are clear indicators that you need to work on your mindset.

You might think that once you have a C-suite role, you feel like you know what you're doing and imposter syndrome isn't a concern. Often, however, the more successful you are, the more likely it can be that you will suffer from imposter syndrome. As an example, Albert Einstein suffered from imposter syndrome, and he also documented it (Buckland, 2017). He's revered as one of the most brilliant scientists of our time, and yet he also suffered from self-doubt.

I was young when I got my first director of finance role at LoveFilm, and my feelings of imposter syndrome were high. This was obvious with my silence within leadership team meetings. I didn't add any value to the decision making, leaving decisions to the executive team and the CFO. I was confident in my day-to-day work, but I wasn't confident outside of the finance department.

By implementing various methods mentioned in this chapter, over time I have built my confidence, and I now feel like a leader. If I notice I'm saying negative things in my head, or talking about issues at home or with colleagues, I generally find that my fears are unfounded. This is also helped by the 'Good feedback' folder I mentioned earlier in this chapter.

Particularly when you are new to a job, you may be shocked by the frequency of your negative self-talk. When you become aware of it, try to turn it around, changing that internal conversation to a more positive one. You're never going to catch all your negative self-talk, because hundreds of thousands of thoughts go through your mind daily. Notice and try to catch the loudest ones, though.

There are benefits to talking to someone if your confidence is really low. These include gaining a different perspective to your own and receiving support from a partner or confidant. If you have a mentor or coach, you could discuss steps you can take to build your confidence with them.

Positive affirmations with conviction can also help. A positive affirmation is the opposite of your negative self-talk. For example, if you catch yourself saying that you aren't very good at speaking up in leadership meetings, simply tell yourself daily that you are and, over time, your confidence will grow. To paraphrase a popular saying: 'Your mind is a garden. Your thoughts are the seeds. The harvest can either be flowers or weeds.' You reap what you sow.

Finding your voice and asking dumb questions

One of my biggest stumbling blocks when moving from a management role to finance a leadership role was finding my voice. I all too often sat in a large meeting and hardly said anything. I was too scared to ask dumb questions or say something silly so thought that not saying anything at all was better. It also didn't help that sometimes I was in a room with fifteen men and no other women, and I found this quite intimidating. However, this imbalance is slowly changing – and it's a different topic.

I thought that, coming from the finance department, I only had the knowledge and authority to talk specifically about numbers and didn't have the right to talk about anything else. This was a huge disservice, though – to myself and my career and also to the business. As a finance leader you have a professional duty to share your opinion and highlight what is working and what isn't.

A big turning point for me was when an impressive female commercial director joined the company. In our leadership meetings she would often ask questions that could be considered dumb, such as how CAC (customer acquisition cost) is defined or what another acronym stood for. I would often welcome these questions, because a lot of the time, they were ones where I didn't know the answer either.

I decided to watch this director as she was highly respected. Every time she asked 'dumb questions', nobody laughed or judged her – they would just answer them. She was clearly challenging the business and challenging the status quo. These weren't dumb questions at all.

She was a good role model for me to learn from. Asking questions, speaking up and challenging the business was a good thing. Every department can get right into the details of their projects and changes and may not see the bigger picture. This is where support functions (like finance) and leaders can help. They can take a step back, see the bigger picture and ensure that all departments are aligned.

The finance team also has access to an incredible amount of data, which can be looked at both from a high level and in detail. Finance also manages the budget, which includes the restrictions on spending and also where the business is going, where the areas of growth are, where the resources are, and the longer-term vision. Using these resources, finance has a lot to contribute to the conversation. People in the business need to hear from you so they too have a strong understanding of finance, especially in startups.

While you focus on contributing to the conversation, don't forget also to listen. Listening to what other people say is an incredibly important part of being a leader, which I'll talk about more in Chapter 3.

Emotional intelligence

Emotional intelligence is another key characteristic of being a good leader. It helps boost self-awareness, self-control, motivation, empathy and social skills, all of which help us become much better leaders. Emotional intelligence has thankfully had more focus over the last few years, particularly as part of leadership and what defines a good leader.

'When dealing with people, remember you are not dealing with creatures of logic, but with creatures of emotion.' This quote, often attributed to American writer and teacher Dale Carnegie, illustrates the importance of emotional intelligence. Dealing with people is probably the most important aspect of a leader's role, so it's vital we focus on our own and others' emotions.

In 2000 Daniel Goleman conducted a Harvard study that determined that emotional intelligence is the baseline for any effective leadership (Goleman, 2000). He noted that there were four distinct characteristics that form emotional intelligence:

1. **Self-awareness:** Understanding who you are, and having self-confidence and an understanding of self-assessment
2. **Self-management:** Being trustworthy, and having self-control and the ability to be motivated to achieve a high level of performance
3. **Social awareness:** Demonstrating understanding, empathy and organisational awareness as well as being more aligned with serving the business
4. **Social skills:** Having strong communication skills, being an advocate for collaboration and being invested in developing other members of the team

If you take your mind back to a manager you had difficulties working with, I'm relatively confident that many of the reasons for those difficulties stemmed from their lack of emotional intelligence.

As culture is important in a smaller company, anything a leader does can reverberate around the business. I can think of leaders who struggled with the concept of emotional intelligence and created a difficult working environment. That environment may have been high-achieving, but it was a challenging and stressful place to work. By being emotionally aware both of yourself and of others, you can lead your team and the business in a more harmonious way. Not only does this culture encourage loyalty and retention, but it makes for a much nicer place to work and ensures you and your team will enjoy coming into the office. The focus will then be on the business's goals rather than the latest drama.

Summary

We have talked about the leadership mindset in this chapter, focusing on confidence and emotional intelligence.

Actions for you:

- Reflect on your past experiences, write them down, and recognise how far you have come in your career.
- Create a 'Good feedback' folder in your email inbox and start filing away all positive feedback you receive.
- Notice negative self-talk. Try to catch it and reverse it.
- Write down some positive affirmations you could say to yourself or use one of the many apps available to help you.

- If you find that your confidence is low, speak to someone such as a partner or confidant, mentor or professional coach.
- Consider what parts of emotional intelligence – from self-awareness, self-management, social awareness and social skills – you already have and whether there are EI skills you would like to develop.
- Go to www.financialleadershipfoundations.com/bookresources for recommendations for further reading on this topic.

3

Communication, Communication, Communication

Strong communication is a significant factor in any leadership role. The amount of communication needed by a finance leader is such a contrast to more junior roles that it warrants its own chapter. In this chapter we will cover the different communication skills and actions you need to perform successfully in your leadership role.

Becoming visible within the business

Visible leadership is when leaders are accessible, approachable and relatable. It's leaders who demonstrate empathy and listen to the team. Leaders who arrange and turn up to meetings and who will have a conversation with you.

Here's an example of the importance of visibility.

CASE STUDY: The invisible CFO

In my second role within the finance industry, I worked under an interesting CFO. I didn't report directly to them; however, it was a small team of just five, so I knew the CFO. The CFO had their own office, and most days their office door remained shut. Because my desk was closest to the CFO's office, other members of the business would often lurk around my desk in the hope of catching the CFO to ask a question. The CFO wasn't available to them either, though, and they rarely appeared from their office.

Each time I had completed the final draft of the monthly reporting, I had to email it to the CFO. I never received any feedback directly from them, but my manager would receive a few bullet points on what needed to be changed. I never had any goals or objectives set, and either my tasks were recurring, or I would receive a last-minute urgent task. I'm not sure the CFO knew anything about me or my life or my career aspirations.

This was a cold and lonely working environment, and I lasted less than two years in the role.

Looking back, I see that this was a good learning experience. I learned what visible leadership *isn't*.

Why visible leadership is important in a startup

Visible leadership has a number of benefits, including the following:

- It helps drive performance.
- It adds to a successful culture.
- It encourages the team to feel engaged, heard and valued.
- It helps with staff retention.
- It improves your personal brand, as others learn who you are and what you stand for, and vice versa.

As a leader you need to be visible not just within your own team but across the entire company. You need to be willing to have conversations outside of the finance team. Face-to-face conversations are the best sort, but they're not always possible as many people work remotely – from home or in other countries. For example, I personally have teams all over the UK, in Indonesia, USA, South Africa and Singapore.

Ensure you turn up to meetings, and that you are visible on video conferencing so people can see you. Whenever possible, meet people where they are based. When you are in the office, walk around talking to your colleagues whenever you have time.

Pre-pandemic, I used to always try and reserve about half an hour in my diary on Fridays for a 'walkaround'. I'd make my way around the office, stopping and engaging in chit chat with department heads, asking how everything was going in their teams. They would often give me a tidbit such as, 'Oh, sales are doing well today, because of an online article/customer services…', or, 'We're struggling today because the phones are down.'

Receiving this information is useful in understanding the business and also helpful in developing relationships. Listening is such a big part of leadership and visible leadership. It helps you understand the issues, goals and motivations of the other departments. This is valuable, especially if you're about to embark on a budgeting process, looking at longer-term goals, or even writing commentary for the monthly reporting.

Managing upwards

Whether you're the CEO reporting to the board, or you're a head of finance and have a CFO, managing upwards is an important part of your role. This is about finding the best way you can work with your superior to ensure you both gain the most possible from the process. It's a significant part of establishing a good relationship with your superior, as it's a two-way relationship.

Communication methods

When working in a junior role, discussion with your superior is around them informing you what to do and you flagging any issues with hitting these deadlines. The relationship is task-orientated.

When you're a leader, the relationship with your superior is different. You need to be more proactive rather than waiting for instructions. It's also worth considering what type of person your superior is and how they like to communicate.

When starting a new relationship with a new startup founder, I ask them how they prefer to communicate, for example, whether they prefer email or message (and if the latter, what type of messaging). Then, over a few weeks, I test out different levels of detail when in face-to-face meetings (generally via video conferencing). I find that if they don't like details, their eyes will glaze over or they'll interrupt me, so I'll switch to delivering information in point form, giving high-level summaries.

Ideally, ensure you have regular catch-ups, scheduled either weekly or biweekly. If they don't set the meetings up, ask if you can. Not all CEOs take the lead here, so you should if needed.

Communication levels

All founders are different. Some founders want to know everything and like to give their views. Others want the bare minimum – they only want to talk about strategy and the commercial side of the business. A great start with a new superior is therefore in identifying their priorities, goals and motivations, as well as their preferred communication style. Work this out either through trial and error or by conversing with longstanding leaders within the business. You can then align your priorities to theirs and anticipate their needs. When you're preparing for a meeting, you can more easily anticipate their questions and therefore be more confident in your answers.

Strengths and weaknesses

Try to understand your superior's strengths and weaknesses as well as your own. You can use their strengths to your advantage and have empathy when it comes to their weaknesses. Also, when you know your own strengths and weaknesses, you can advocate for work you are best suited to.

In the world of startups and scaleups, many founders are also first-time CEOs and potentially need to lean on the finance leader for guidance. Helping them understand how you can support them and why your role is important for growth maximisation and risk minimisation is important for your relationship.

Efficiency

It's ideal not to hesitate in communicating, especially when something's about to go wrong. I have fallen foul of this in the past.

CASE STUDY: Speaking up as soon as possible

I remember discovering an issue within operations that had affected financial results. I didn't pick up this issue until a couple of months into the role.

I decided to spend time with the details and the team, to work out the status quo and which process had fallen. Once I had all the facts, I spoke to the founder about the issue and how it was going to affect the financials.

This founder liked details, and they were annoyed that they were informed at a late date, meaning they couldn't do anything about it. In hindsight, knowing what the issue was and also knowing that this founder likes details, I should have informed them much earlier in the process.

Whenever there's some bad news, *always* communicate that as early as possible, allowing the superior an opportunity to solve or mitigate that problem. The last thing they want is to be told the bad news when it's too late for them to be able to do anything about it.

Proactive problem solving

With problem solving, particularly when you want your superior's opinion, always offer solutions with your recommendations. If there are multiple solutions, you can list these solutions and give your recommendation. The superior can then decide if they agree with your recommendation or not.

Never come to a meeting at leadership level with a problem and no potential solution. It also helps if you are mindful of your superior's goals, so your proposed solutions are aligned with their motivations.

Setting expectations

I like to work hard, and I have a tendency to tell people I can help them to complete an unrealistic amount of work in a short time frame. The key word here is *unrealistic*.

Many times in the past, I have told various colleagues around the business that the team and I can deliver a certain piece of work that will add considerable value to them and their business decision making, which is great for building that relationship.

I have then told another five colleagues the same thing.

Then I've realised it's quarter end, a board meeting is imminent, and the founder has just asked for an additional scenario for a particular investor.

Aaargh!

The team and I have then been forced to spend *many* late nights working so we could deliver all the promised tasks, to avoid losing trust within the business.

What I have learned – and what I practise now – is to plan and set more realistic expectations with businesses. Things won't work out well if you always overpromise and underperform. It will be a negative experience for your colleagues, and it's stressful for both you and your team. It just isn't a great way to work.

Remember: as a leader, you are judged on your output, not on how hard you work.

In *The First 90 Days,* a book I recommend, author Michael D Watkins writes, 'Clarify expectations early and often. Begin managing expectations from the moment you consider taking a new role' (Watkins, 2013). He continues to explain that you should focus on expectations from as early as the interview process. If there are serious issues at this new company, you'll run into difficulties if your superior demands rapid solutions. Instead, Watkins advises to uncover all issues as soon as possible and to lower unrealistic expectations. After that, you need to keep checking that your superior hasn't changed their expectations, which is especially important if you're transitioning from a different company and don't yet fully understand the culture and politics of this new business.

It's much safer to under-promise and overperform than vice versa.

Seeking feedback

If you can, seek regular feedback. If you get the right kind of feedback (constructive), it can help you to develop your leadership skills, especially if you start seeing recurring themes in that feedback.

It can be hard to ask for feedback, especially when you know it's going to include some criticism. It's a bit of a cliché, but feedback truly is a gift, helping you improve your performance. It also isn't always easy to give feedback, especially constructive feedback.

I still remember criticisms I have received in the past, and I know that some points highlighted genuine weaknesses of mine. This feedback has therefore helped me understand who I am. It has helped me identify gaps that I need to fill, either by learning and improving in those areas, particularly if they're softer skills; or ensuring that I can enlist help from the team if they're stronger in that area.

It is also worthwhile actively giving feedback, especially to your team. I'll go through team building in a later chapter, but feedback is a two-way street.

Talking finance to non-finance folk

I'm sure I'm not the only one who has tried to talk about different accounting topics, where others either don't understand what I'm saying, or they aren't vaguely interested in listening. You need to be mindful in this line of work that not everybody will be as financially literate as you are.

Being an accountant – or a 'bean counter' – does have some negative connotations, particularly socially, when someone asks you what you do for a living, and you prep yourself quickly for the jokes they'll react with. I was once at a small comedy show, and we were unfortunately too close to the front for comfort. I was asked by the comedian what I did for a living. *Oh, no!* This was decades ago, so I was quite young and simply replied that I was a business student rather than prompting a barrage of derogatory jokes. I was then mocked for being a drug dealer, but I thought I got off more lightly that if I'd told the comedian I was an accountant!

These social feelings towards accountants often carry over into business, particularly at a startup, where there are many junior members of the team that don't understand what an accountant does and perhaps only understand the social cues.

The higher you climb up the corporate ladder, the more often you'll be speaking to non-finance people. In startups or scaleups, you might be the only finance team member, or there might just be a small team, and you'll therefore often be communicating with people outside of the finance department.

In general, I find that diverse industries have different levels of accounting knowledge around the business. Working for a FinTech, it almost feels as if the team outside of the finance department are more financially literate than us! Retail, however, can be the other end of the scale.

I am currently a trustee for a charity, and the difference is even more pronounced. The CEO and I are the only two that care about the numbers. Everybody else just leaves the accounting to us and doesn't mind what the numbers say, as long there is enough cash in the bank to conduct the charitable work.

I use three methods to encourage engagement:

1. Motivation
2. Education
3. Pictures and stories

1. Motivation

Sometimes the best way to start a conversation with one person or a group is to find out what their motivations are. If you're addressing their needs, they're more likely to be engaged in the conversation.

CASE STUDY: Engaging over concerns

I remember talking to a group of junior sales reps, and I kicked off a discussion about their OKRs (objectives and key results – a method of setting operational goals), inviting them to talk about their main concerns. Those weren't financial; however, elements of either financial statements or KPIs were relevant.

By taking on their concerns, I could align their OKRs to certain elements of the financial statements or their KPIs so they could see the connection. This piqued their interest, encouraged them to be engaged and allowed them to see how their actions and goals affected the entire business.

After this, they were more engaged with the bigger picture and what I had to say. This process also gave me feedback, plus visibility on what had been happening behind the scenes.

---

2. Education

I have held 'lunch and learn' sessions with members of my teams. I've held these at lunchtime, for whoever wants to turn up and learn about finance and to understand business finances a bit better. This is a great way of introducing the company's financial KPIs. I would often present what the board is interested in – such as revenue and CAC – explaining what they are and then applying that information to how the team see the business.

Keep accounting terms for the finance team and for the auditors. Take the jargon out of what you're presenting/communicating. It may feel like using clever terms will impress your audience, but it does the opposite. Being able to talk about a complex topic in simple terms is more impressive, as long as you aren't patronising.

3. Pictures and stories

Generally, if I'm presenting to a large group, I use stories to get my point across. It's also useful to use real-life company examples, as they can be easier to understand. For example, you could use a successful process change in your company or that implemented by a well-known brand or competitor.

Using pictures is another option that will help your message be understood. When presenting, you will need to consider whether you can best impart the knowledge by telling a story, showing pictures, or both.

Pictures such as charts and graphs make it much easier to convey a message than a table full of numbers. Just ensure that the charts aren't too complex. Below are a few examples.

Often, simplicity is key to tell a true narrative, as illustrated by the amusing pie chart below.

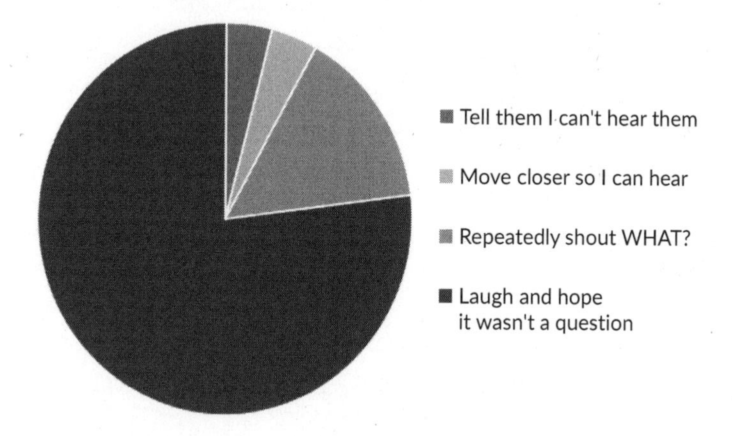

What I do when I can't hear someone

In comparison, the chart below looks impressive, but what is it trying to tell you? There are too many variables, and it's hard to work out what the presenter is trying to convey.

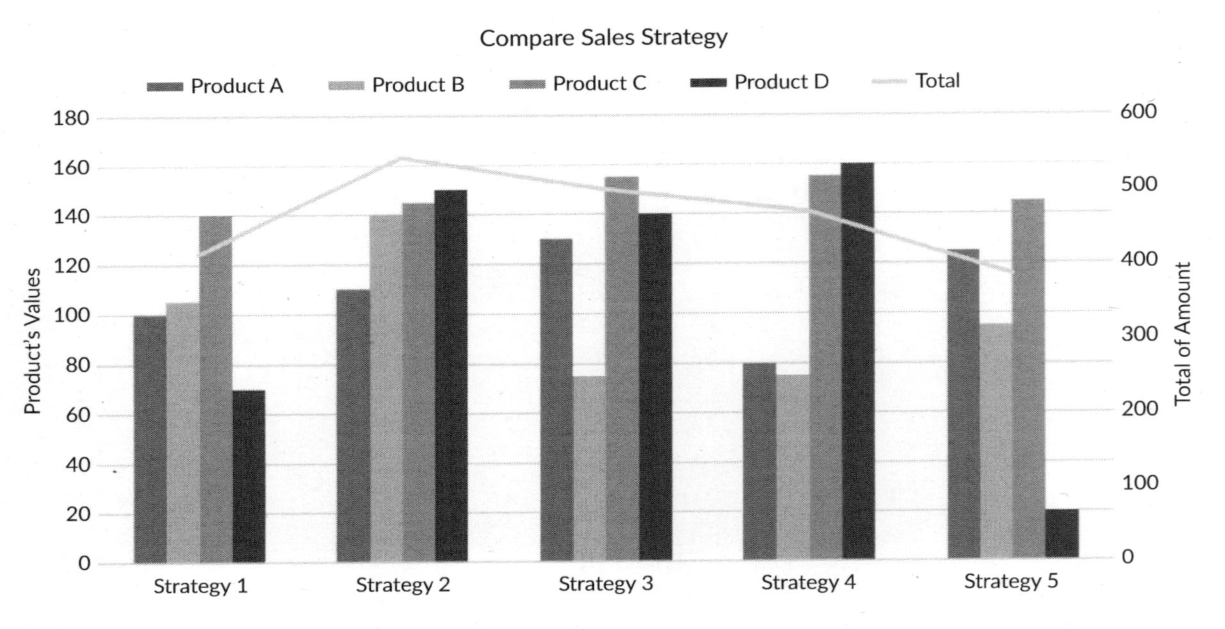

An overly complicated chart

Summary

We've talked about communication in this chapter, focusing on visibility, managing upwards, setting expectations and talking to non-finance people.

Actions for you:

- Look at how you're communicating with your team and other key members around the business. Do you need to set up weekly, biweekly or monthly meetings?
- Find out how your founder/CEO responds to different types of communication.
- Work out your superior's motivations. Keep an ongoing list of what you want to talk to them about so you're always prepared for your catch-ups.
- Add 'request feedback' to your list of discussion points.
- Before presenting a challenge or issue, think it through. What are the possible solutions? What are the pros and cons of each solution?
- Consider offering 'lunch and learn' or educational sessions around the business to gain engagement from people who are less financially literate.

4

The Role Of A CFO In A Startup Or Scaleup

A good understanding of the CFO role and finance function in a startup or scaleup is important as there are more roles and responsibilities than you have with management accounts. The makeup of the finance function is also changing, with constant improved automation and the introduction of artificial intelligence (AI).

The role of the CFO and finance function

A 2023 *Forbes* article captures the essence of the CFO role in an analogy of a road-rally navigator (Kellerman, 2023). George Kellerman says that the CFO acts like the navigator who rides alongside while the CEO steers the business through the race.

While the CEO keeps their eyes on the road, the CFO-navigator reads a topographical map, keeping track of time and landmarks and saying things like, '500 yards ahead, there's a steep slope and a hard left.' Their teamwork and mutual trust prevent the business from crashing.

I love this analogy. Essentially, CFO responsibilities extend well beyond the spreadsheet. On the surface, the finance team's focus is on numbers – cashflow, budgets and profitability – but they deal with much more. Other responsibilities include risk management, strategic planning and negotiations.

I will go through all the above elements of a CFO role in detail over the coming chapters. First, though, it is worthwhile stepping back and reviewing what a CEO or founder in a startup or scaleup wants from their CFO.

As a fractional CFO – employed part-time to give strategic advice and support – I hear firsthand the reasons for founders wanting to hire me. These include:

- Filling a gap left by an outgoing CFO
- Providing help in preparing for a fundraise
- Giving the founder a sparring partner or a strategic partner
- Someone coming in with lots of experience, understanding the business model and

identifying the potential opportunities as well as the potential threats

- Employing someone to help the CEO maximise growth and minimise risks

This demonstrates what a founder initially demands from their CFO; the role builds up from there. The CFO role is multilayered. The CFO needs to be a finance guru as well as a risk assessor, business forecaster and strategic adviser. The ability to balance between these different elements of the role, all while maintaining control of the company's finances and cashflow, is what makes a truly great CFO.

How AI will change the finance function

Post-ChatGPT there has been much discussion on AI replacing all existing jobs. If the changes in accounting software over the last five years are anything to go by, AI will continue to change our roles significantly. We need to ensure that we grow and learn with these changing times.

A detailed report by the World Economic Forum reveals that, largely due to the improvement of technology, demand for various financial roles will significantly reduce in 2025 (World Economic Forum, 2020). Those include roles in accounting, bookkeeping and payroll clerks; accountants and auditors; and financial analysts.

As the world becomes more digital, accountants need to evolve to keep up with the changes in technology. The traditional roles and responsibilities of accountants are being changed by automation, AI and machine learning. This has led to many concerns about the future of accounting and whether the profession will remain relevant in the years to come.

This concern has unfortunately already hit the demand of university students in a big way. According to *The CPA Journal*, there has been a marked decline in the number of students choosing to study accounting (Burke, Polimeni, 2023). The article highlights: 'As a direct result of enrolment declines in accounting programmes, candidates sitting for the CPA exam have also decreased, from 48,004 first-time candidates in 2016 to 32,188 in 2021, a drop of 33%.'

I agree that the current role of finance departments is going to be significantly disrupted.

As I have seen over the last fifteen years, the junior roles within the finance function have reduced. When I started working as a financial controller at LoveFilm in 2006, in my team I had an accounts payable clerk, accounts receivable clerk, payroll and bank reconciliation clerk, and an assistant accountant. All four roles are now combined into that of a finance manager. This role will continue to be automated over the coming years and will probably disappear as management reports are forecasted to be prepared by a click of a button.

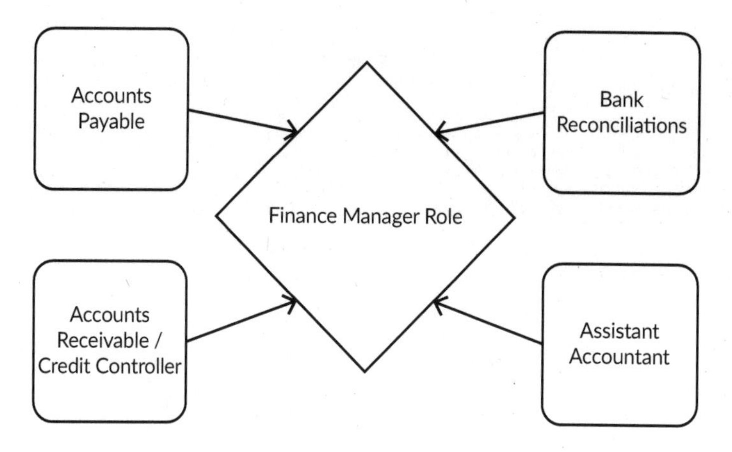

The finance manager role

Although this may all sound doom and gloom, I have also seen a rise in demand of the accountant in different areas outside of financial operations, particularly for the CFO within businesses.

Also, with continued increases in financial regulation, global businesses and internationalisation, there will be:

- New regulations that will probably sit under finance, such as ESG (environmental, social and governance) reporting
- Higher audit requirements
- Earlier due diligence requirements from investors
- A better understanding of information that finance functions can provide to business leaders

The finance function responsibilities may reduce within financial operations, but they will increase significantly in other areas. The role is becoming more strategic, rather than just number crunching as it was in the past. However, educating yourself is more important than ever to ensure that your skills remain relevant and that you move with the times.

Being proactive rather than reactive

As our roles change – due to automation and AI, and also in moving up from a management role to a leadership role – there is a strong need to be more proactive rather than reactive. As the team's routine tasks become more automated, more time and resources are available that can be dedicated to value-adding tasks.

Defining proactive and reactive

Particularly in startups and scaleups, things move quickly, and often break – for example, a website goes down or a key supplier pulls out last minute. Dealing with the aftermath of this is a reactionary response – you're reacting to a situation or an issue, or *fighting fires*.

For example, after payroll was paid, you found out from HR (or, more likely, from the employees themselves) that their commission payments were wrong. As a reactionary response, you and your team need to check what has happened, calculate the difference and then make an additional payment today. The team will need to communicate the work and findings to all stakeholders.

The benefits of being proactive

In relation to the above example, a proactive task would be reviewing your processes and noticing that the payroll process isn't watertight. Perhaps there aren't relevant reviews, and the commission calculations aren't checked. Once you identify this, you improve the process to ensure that issues such as wrong commission payments never arise. You have identified a risk and put processes in place to mitigate them.

Another example of being proactive as a finance leader is looking at opportunities outside of the finance department for growth and to mitigate against risks. Looking at a range of potential outcomes or options during the forecasting process is the perfect time to be more proactive in business outcomes. Look for ways that you can help the business drive the actions in the business to maximise opportunities.

Deciding which relationships you should own

Outside your business partners and the internal team, which relationships should you own as a finance leader in a startup or scaleup? These fall under the following wide range of areas:

- **Banking:** There should be multiple bank accounts within your parent entity or the company that you're working with. Other financial institutions could be foreign exchange providers and card or credit card providers. Sometimes the cards are with a bank account, but often you can use companies that have better portals or better rewards.
- **Tax:** Tax accountants that help you with year-end returns, VAT providers, R&D tax returns, and general advice such as transfer pricing would fall under your remit. Often you may have a different tax accountant per region, depending on how big your company is and how big a firm you want to employ. A large multinational company, for example, would hire a Tier 1 accounting firm so that the tax planning can cover all jurisdictions, but this comes at a price a startup or scaleup cannot afford.
- **Tax offices:** This is region-specific, eg HMRC, ATO or IRS. Any correspondence with these departments will fall within the finance department.
- **Audits:** If relevant, overseeing the audit could be your responsibility. Either your company is big enough to require an audit as per the

country's legislation, or more likely than not, the shareholders may require one.

- **Payroll:** You will own the relationship with the company's payroll suppliers. That will include a payroll bureau, if not in-house, and also payroll software, pension, 401K or superannuation providers, and often staff benefits such as health insurance.
- **Company registry:** This includes Companies House, ASIC, Delaware or company registry for each region. Often company secretarial duties will fall on the finance leader – so just be aware of who is managing the administration requirements of each company.
- **Regulators:** This generally refers to FinTech and InsureTech businesses such as the FCA in the UK, Federal Reserve in the USA, and APRA or ASIC in Australia. Your company may also be regulated under different regulators, so check who is managing this in your company.
- **Lenders:** This includes venture debt, asset finance or any other institutions that you borrow from.
- **Technical support companies:** Finance software, SaaS and similar support companies will normally be managed by the finance leader rather than by tech.

- **Employment lawyers and commercial contract lawyers:** If there isn't an established legal department, often the legal management could fall under finance or the CFO.
- **Estate brokers, landlords and property consultants:** This could also fall under finance. Ideally, this is allocated to office administration within operations, but not always.
- **HR:** HR operations may fall under finance until there's an established HR function. This may include employee benefit provision, culture surveys, or in-house communication education.
- **Data:** This includes GDPR consultants and other data security concerns. Data security may also fall under tech and GDPR within legal, but I've seen these suppliers come under finance.

You may have responsibility for other relationships, depending on your role. For example, if you manage procurement, your key suppliers and merchant suppliers will fall under your jurisdiction. Insurance brokers as well as credit insurers also often sit with the head of finance.

When starting in a finance leadership role, it is vital to confirm from the start which relationships you own by having this conversation with the founder.

I'm often asked by either the board or the founder/CEO for recommendations from my network. This could be for other professionals such as insurance brokers or lawyers, or for financial institutions. Make sure that you are always adding to your network of contacts, including suppliers who can help you, and other CFOs who can give you recommendations for your situation.

Working with boards and investors

Before we look at your relationship with boards and investors, I want to give you a quick overview on the makeup of the board, particularly for startups and scaleup businesses.

Board members

The makeup of a board for a startup or scaleup is different from that of a large corporate or a listed entity. In general, the founder and the CEO (often but not always the same person) are on the board, and they are often the only executives, unless there is a full-time CFO within the business. If there is, the CFO is often also part of the board. The board would also include the lead investor or investors, depending on how many fundraisers there have been and how big the individual investors are.

Non-executive directors and advisers can also form part of the board. At this early stage, they are unpaid.

If an investor has invested heavily into the business, they may also want to have a board seat, which will be part of their condition of their investment. They may want voting rights, to be privy to confidential information and to have their opinion heard on the direction of the company. These requests may not come to fruition for each investor – they will be negotiated on throughout. During the funding round, the existing board and founders may restrict the number of the board members as it can become too difficult. Especially if you are trying to drive a business that's nimble and fast growing, the more members you have on the board, the harder it is to find consensus and answer everyone's questions.

The board can also have what is known as a *silent observer*. This is somebody who can attend and watch but doesn't contribute to a board meeting. An example is when board access is negotiated during a fundraise. Either the investor decides they want to be a silent observer and comes to an agreement with the board, or they wanted to get a board seat but have compromised by becoming a silent observer.

The board can have a company secretary, who could be the business's general counsel. Often, though, in the early stages one of the other board members or a finance team member would take on the role of secretary, especially if there's no in-house counsel.

If there is more than one entity within the company group, the main board would be for the parent entity and would often have between five to seven members.

The board works for the shareholders and stakeholders and will make decisions based on this responsibility. Board members will be interested in overseeing the business strategy, the management of the business, and the accuracy of the financial statements.

The topics the board will be interested in are:

1. Strategy
2. People
3. Reputation
4. Finance
5. Compliance

1. Strategy

The board will be looking at strategy from both macro and micro perspectives, and they are also interested in competitors, USP, the product range and what's happening with the customers. The real details are talked about outside of the boardroom, so the board will be looking at topics from a high level.

2. People

The board will consider if the right people are in the most senior positions as well as throughout the rest of the company. They will be considering whether the right culture is being met, and if the people being employed by the company are going to be able to implement strategy.

3. Reputation

As the board see things at a high level, they can challenge any actions if they believe they may harm the reputation or brand of the business.

4. Finance

The board will look at the monthly or quarterly financial statements, cashflow, and the different decisions around cash. For example, if you decide to take on venture debt or start a new fundraise, those usually must be approved by the board. The annual budget and any potential audit will also need to be reported to the board. As the company grows, there may be a separate audit committee.

5. Compliance

This covers regulations, risks and compliance, with a focus also on legislation and on ensuring the business adheres to the relevant laws. Compliance is particularly important for financial services. Often, as a company gets larger, you will have a separate regulatory and governance board that feeds in to the main board.

Your role in relation to the board

How much interaction you have with the board is at the discretion of the CEO. Some may want you to get heavily involved in their investor relations, either wanting your help or for you to own those relationships. At early-stage startups, it's more likely that the CEO would want to own those relationships, though, largely because members of the board are advisers and help the CEO on how to grow the business. However, when you bring on larger venture capitalists (VCs) at the later stages, the CEO often wants you to support those with investor relationships.

When there is a fundraise, the founders need to be careful in who to choose as investors and potential board members. They need people who will add value to the board, to discussions and to the direction of the business. Sometimes it's a worthwhile exercise to work out what gaps in knowledge the board has and seek to fill those gaps with any additions. Often the chairman will do this alongside the founder, but the CFO may also be asked for input.

With early-stage businesses, the leaders within the business prepare the board pack or any materials needed by the CEO. The board pack is then presented at the board meeting, either by the CEO alone or with help from the business leaders. I will cover what to include in board reporting in Chapter 8.

Most large investors will require summarised financial statements as well. All these requirements will be clarified in the shareholder agreement.

Whenever there is a fundraise, always ask for the signed shareholder agreement so you can see what is required by the finance function. Items to look out for when reviewing the shareholder agreement include:

- **Financial reporting:** Including specifying reports, how often they should be sent, and sometimes even relevant deadlines
- **Annual audits:** Which month these need to be completed and the time frame
- **Insurance policies:** The most common being directors' and officers' (D&O) insurance (how big they want the liability to cover themselves as members of the board), and key man insurance policies
- **Annual budget reviews:** Which also often have a deadline, such as thirty days before year end
- **Any restrictions or suspensive conditions:** Such as limiting trading activities of the founder(s) or other key shareholders

Working with third parties

When managing third-party suppliers, there are two areas of consideration, particularly for a CFO or finance director and for a startup or scaleup:

1. Key supplier risks
2. Third-party relationships managed by the CFO

1. Key supplier risks

This is about how the company's performance, reputation or compliance could be put at risk by a supplier, for example, operational issues, their tech going offline, cyber risks and even going out of business or deciding to cease trading with you. You need to establish who your large or key suppliers are – the ones that you rely on to make sales and keep the company afloat.

CASE STUDY: Backup needed

The UK had to deal with a post-Brexit world straight after a pandemic. I had one client who relied heavily on a goods supplier in the EU. Unfortunately, this presented key supplier risk – the company had only one supplier, which they had used for many years, so that supplier was a key component of their sales.

This company struggled during the pandemic and were keen to get back on their feet post-Covid. However, they hadn't factored in the fact that the border between the UK and the EU would be in disarray for almost six months, due to the new Brexit rules. Their supplier couldn't get their goods into the UK in time – some containers were stuck at customs for months.

The client has now mitigated this supplier risk by having more suppliers in different locations, but it was tough going for quite some time.

Supplier failures can be related to goods and services. If your company is heavily reliant on the cloud or one piece of software to remain in operation, what is your backup plan? This can also relate to quality risks, particularly with products, although quality issues can also happen with services. If you're not receiving the service you require, can the business easily switch, or is this company or service too embedded?

Reviewing all your suppliers and making an assessment based on how important they are to the company, consider the likelihood that they could fall over or breach another risk such as quality. This is important. You can mitigate some of that risk by developing a stronger relationship, reviewing the contracts or ensuring that there isn't one point of failure, particularly with key suppliers.

2. Third-party relationships managed by the CFO

As a CFO, you should aim to meet with the third parties that you manage – finance providers such as auditors and insurers – every six months. With the more critical third parties, such as banks, credit insurers and payroll providers, consider quarterly meetings. This gives you a chance to develop a good working relationship with them.

It's also ideal to update suppliers on the current business trajectory, particularly if a lot of growth is expected. This update provides a communication channel to give both positive feedback on what's working and anything that's not working so well and needs improvement. They may reciprocate with feedback to you, and they will have the opportunity to update you on any additional services they're planning on rolling out that may be of interest to your company.

After you have made a list of your third-party relationships, you might find that you have outgrown some of your suppliers or that they have some gaps in their supply chains, meaning they can't provide what you require. For example, you may have moved to a new region and need new or better tax advisers; or following a fundraise, you may be required to submit audited accounts. In this case, a tender process will need to be run to find potential suppliers.

Summary

In this chapter I have discussed the role of the startup or scaleup finance function and CFO, including how

AI may change the future; relationships that you own; and how to deal with investors, boards and third parties.

Actions for you:

- Make a note of all relationships that you own or potentially own. Discuss this with your founder/CEO to ensure that you're all aligned.
- Work with your founder/CEO on how much they want you to be involved in investor relations.
- Get a copy of the most recent shareholder agreement and ensure that all requirements have been met.
- Keep a record of who is on the board – this will need to be reported in the annual financial statements.
- Ensure you're aware of all investor requirements in the shareholder agreement.
- Make a list of all third parties, including contact names and details. Work out what is working well and who you may replace, especially as the company grows.
- Implement or encourage third-party key supplier risks within your organisation and with your finance suppliers.
- Go through a tender process if you need to acquire new third-party relationships.

PART TWO

KEEPING THE LIGHTS ON

This is the second part of the Financial Leadership Fundamentals Framework. Before we can start going through analysis and adding value, we have to ensure that the baseline is correct. With or without a financial controller, a CFO needs to ensure that the baseline is accurate.

5

The Boring Stuff You Can't Ignore

The first important point of Part Two is understanding the baseline and the core numbers. When working with new clients, the initial task is due diligence, to ensure everything is where it should be. When taking on a new role, due diligence should be the first thing you do too.

The importance of a good baseline

I remember speaking to a founder earlier this year who was complaining about their prior CFO, who had been asked to leave the business. *Yikes!*

This hadn't come about because the CFO wasn't good at strategy. Instead, it was due to the management accounts. The leadership team would find mistakes, so no one trusted the numbers or any analysis that was based on this data.

Management accounts and a clean balance sheet might not be the most glamorous task on your to-do list. However, this is where you can showcase your understanding of the business and any analysis skills (which I will go through in later chapters). Unfortunately, it can also kill your career if you don't give your core numbers the dedication and focus required.

Trust is an essential part of leadership and career progression in finance. The quickest way to kill trust with your colleagues, board, investors and leadership team is by producing reports that have an inconsistent baseline.

The most common causes for numbers becoming untrustworthy are as follows:

- **The numbers keep moving.** This is often the result of the general ledger remaining open long after month end has 'closed'. Do you close off a month end and then forget to lock the general ledger? Or isn't this process within your month-end schedule? If so, you may find that the numbers keep moving.
- **Items are posted inconsistently around the ledger.** This happens when the actuals aren't matched properly to the forecast or budget.

We'll go through this in much more detail in Part Three.

- **The balance sheet isn't reconciled properly on a regular basis.** A clean balance sheet is an essential part of a strong foundation, largely because any discrepancy will need to be recognised. You then need to push the variance through the P&L, affecting the month-end results. If this happens often, the P&L will make less sense and the trust in your numbers and your team's abilities will be put into question.
- **Accrual accounting methods aren't used correctly.** In general, all businesses use accrual accounting; however, cash accounting can sometimes still be used in part. I have seen firsthand inconsistencies here, especially with startups who just have a bookkeeper. If accrual accounting is used for some of the P&L and not all, it's inconsistent.
- **The management accounts or financial reports are hard to read and include too much unimportant detail.** Presentation is important; we'll cover this in Part Three.

CASE STUDY: Accrual accounting

I once had a client who didn't account for their inventory via accrual accounting methods. Their gross margin was all over the place, as they recognised cost of sales only when they made the payment. Their bookkeeper, however, used accrual accounting for overheads – not very useful.

The board wasn't happy with this P&L, and we were brought in to fix it.

The best way to check that your baseline is accurate is to conduct an internal audit.

Internal audits

An internal audit is the ideal first task when you are starting a new role. It will give you a good understanding of the financial health of the business. You cannot start implementing changes or making any decisions after looking at the numbers if the numbers are wrong. Bad data leads to bad decisions.

It's your responsibility to ensure that you understand the financial acumen of the numbers. Is the balance sheet clean, so you can understand the commercials just by looking at the financial statements? Or are there a few issues? This is a more likely scenario with a small business (and a large business!).

An internal audit has a few functions, namely:

- Review of financial reporting and numbers
- Monitoring internal controls

- Risk management
- Review of compliance and regulations
- Corporate governance
- Review of operating activities

If you had an internal audit function, all these items would be under your jurisdiction. However, startup and scaleups don't have these resources and so the audit is up to the finance leader, the general counsel and the COO. If you have worked in an audit firm before, you might be familiar with this.

How to conduct an internal audit

I recommend starting with:

1. **Financial audit:** Reviewing the finance numbers and KPIs
2. **Internal controls:** Identifying what they are and any gaps
3. **Regulations:** Finding out if there are specific requirements for your industry
4. **Financial operations:** Reviewing the current processes

You can expand this, especially if you are working for a regulated entity and therefore compliance and corporate governance are higher priorities. As a minimum, though, the four I'm going to discuss should be the ones you look at in the beginning. We'll also discuss risk management within Chapter 6.

1. Financial audit

The initial focus is the balance sheet, where the skeletons will be hiding – it's where you will find many problems.

If you have conducted any type of audit before, or you have a tight month-end process, this will be familiar to you. However, it's worth summarising here that we want to confirm every single item on the balance sheet with an external resource.

Establish which period to focus on first, and conduct a high-level check on every single account on the balance sheet. Make sure you don't miss any account, as that will no doubt be the one that gives you trouble further down the line. You need to get a good upfront understanding.

If any accounts don't reconcile or you just can't work out where they come from, this is a good place to start digging, investigating and ultimately reconciling. If anything needs to be fixed, nine times out of ten it must go through the P&L.

The next step of a financial audit is to look at the P&L. I'll cover the actual P&L structure and how it can add value in Chapter 8. Here the focus is to check that the P&L is being managed correctly. I would review the trends and look for any peaks or troughs that can't be explained.

Ensure that all accounts are using proper accrual accounting methods rather than cash accounting. For example, I worked with a team where accrual methods were used for everything except for the sales team commissions. What the sales team was paid each month was within the P&L. However, the sales team paid their monthly commissions one month in arrears, so a high revenue month could have a low sales commission cost in the P&L and vice versa.

I would also look to see if any transactions are being posted differently each month. For example, I have seen freight and courier costs within cost of sales (CoS), and then couriers as part of overheads, giving an odd gross margin.

Finally, I would check various percentage calculations – gross margin, contribution margins, operating margins and group costs – each as a percentage of revenue. Are these relatively stable, or are they variable?

Check that the cashflow statement balances, ie the cashflow ending cash balance is the same as the balance sheet cash balance in the same period. A lack of balance here is quite a common error.

Ensure that there aren't multiple definitions of or calculations for one figure. For example, a common problem is different customer numbers, depending on which department is reporting. The customer numbers that the finance team report may be different to the sales team and different again to the customer services team.

Look at all the internal and external deadlines, ensuring they have been met. These include internal deadlines such as business reporting (weekly or monthly), payroll deadlines, how quickly the management accounts are being finalised, the team meetings, shareholder reporting requirements, other weekly reporting, and board reporting. External deadlines include the statutory and legislative requirements for each company.

Other external reporting – for example, reporting to key suppliers or credit insurance – may be specific to the company. Banking or financing partners may also want quarterly reporting due to a loan facility or if the company is holding client monies.

That is largely the financial aspect of the audit. I also go through KPIs in detail in Chapter 8.

2. Internal controls

Any gaps within internal controls may have been highlighted while investigating issues within the financial information. There is usually an issue within the financial reconciliation due to a lack in internal controls. I will be going through internal controls in detail in the next chapter. For now, I want to highlight three key areas that can provide quick wins:

1. **Procurement and accounts payable:** What is the current process for managing suppliers and the invoices that come in and are ready for payment?
2. **Payroll:** Are there any automations and reconciliations? Implement controls quickly here if they are lacking.
3. **Revenue:** Is there a triangular reconciliation, and what is the process of ensuring that revenue is accurate? Does your sales data = revenue = cash?

My number-one check as soon as possible is to find out how the finance team change supplier bank details when a request comes in from a supplier. A fraudulent change of bank details request is the most common type of fraud I have seen. Stringent controls need to be in place to mitigate this risk (see Chapter 6 for further detail).

3. Regulations

This point is specific to each industry. The most detailed and complicated I have dealt with are FCA reporting requirements for financial service businesses. If you have just started in a new industry, it's a good idea to discuss regulations with the CEO, the existing finance team and even your network to find out if there are regulations your company needs to adhere to.

There may also be other financial requirements such as financial covenants if the company has agreed to a debt facility. Some large commercial agreements may also have covenants. Find all the agreements, discover exactly what those financial covenants are, and ensure each month that the company meets them and is projected to fall within those covenants in future periods.

4. Financial operations

When reviewing internal controls and their effectiveness, it's also worth reviewing how good the actual process is and how well operations are running. For example, with accounts payable and receivable revenue recognition, how manual or automatic is this process? Is it consistent throughout the company? Is there a policy that everyone follows? If there isn't, this is probably an area that you need to streamline.

Risk registers

Many small businesses don't have a risk register, and they perhaps may not need one in the early stages, as it's more important that the company is nimble, has a good product and focuses on growing. However, an understanding of the risks needs to be established by the business. It's a good idea to implement a high-level risk register, as it encourages the leadership team to think about what risks their department and the business as a whole have. It allows a business to mitigate any of these risks, where possible.

For example, in 2018 to 2019 in the UK, Brexit would have been on many risk registers, particularly for retailers and distributors, and there's not much they could do about Brexit not happening. However, companies could potentially mitigate this risk by opening a warehouse on the continent for distribution, rather than distributing from the UK and having to deal with customs issues.

A risk register is usually managed by finance, operations, legal, or risk departments (at a finance services company). Raise the option of a risk register to your leadership team. The board may even ask for a risk register to be established.

Audit frequency

As I mentioned right at the beginning of this chapter, an internal audit is something you'll want to do when starting in a new role, whether that role is with the company you've been working with for years or at a brand-new company. Even if you've worked for a company for a long time and you're in a new finance director role, it's worthwhile revisiting the internal audit. This will allow you to work out where the risks are, what's high risk, what's low risk, and the areas that need to be tackled first. It will also help you identify your priorities, say over the next six to twelve months.

After the audit, ask your finance function to reconcile the balance sheet quarterly at a minimum, and ideally monthly. Bank reconciliations are non-negotiable – they must reconcile regularly. Other accounts on the balance sheet that move regularly such as accruals, prepayments, and control and payroll accounts should also be monthly. If you have a resources issue, the rest of the balance sheet can be completed quarterly.

Summary

We have talked about why a good baseline is essential, what an internal audit is, how to conduct one and how often it should be done, as well as about risk registers.

Actions for you:

- If you haven't conducted an internal audit before, do it this week! Cover financial audit, internal controls, regulations and financial operations at a minimum.
- Ensure your finance team reconcile the high-risk items, constantly moving items monthly and reviewing the whole balance sheet at least quarterly.
- Ensure there is a finance calendar that has all deadlines and that it is kept updated.
- Conduct internal audit reviews that will take a couple of days. If you have this booked in your calendar in advance, you will more likely complete them. If you ignore balance sheet reconciliations, this will become an issue for you further down the line.
- Allow time quarterly to review all elements of an internal audit, to ensure the baseline is kept in check.

6
Risks And Controls

As discussed in prior chapters, a big part of the finance leader's role is to manage risks. Processes and controls are tools that can be used to mitigate financial risks.

External risks

An area that requires finance to manage the external risks is with external suppliers. The business must also deal with many other direct external risks such as hacking and cyber risk, stock and property. However, the mitigation against these risks generally lies with tech and operations. The finance leader should ensure that risk mitigation processes are in place, as well as the right insurance policy, but they will not be directly responsible for putting these processes in place.

I have seen a few fraud instances related to external supplier risk in the last ten years. Thankfully, they were all with different companies.

With the first company, an invoice created by a fraudster was emailed to the operations department. Not only were the bank details not checked, but the invoice also hadn't been properly approved. In this example, £4,000 was paid to a fraudster and had to be written off.

In the second example, a regular monthly invoice of £2,500 arrived. The invoice was legitimate, but a fraudster had emailed all supplier contacts within the supplier's system with a change of bank details request. The bookkeeper changed the bank details without going through any process, and £2,500 was sent to the fraudster. The realisation that this was incorrect only happened when the supplier chased up their £2,500 debt. Again, this amount had to be written off, and new policies were swiftly put in place.

As a word of warning: I've also seen similar examples with insignificant amounts. My favourite example was when I managed a finance team in Germany. The junior accountant of that team received a WhatsApp message, supposedly from me (under my name and with a picture of me that was scraped from the internet). The message said that I was in a board meeting talking about a confidential M&A (merger and acquisition), and we needed to transfer €15,000 to the lawyer's escrow account rather than to the usual bank account. The message also said this was highly confidential, so the recipient should not talk to anyone about it. Thankfully, this junior accountant had the foresight to speak to the financial controller, who in turn emailed me to check. They had been convinced it was legitimate, but it wasn't, and this fraudster wasn't paid.

Payment security is one of the first controls I check with a new company. If there are no controls in place, we look at methods to mitigate this risk.

Fraudsters are incredibly sophisticated and continually come up with new methods to defraud companies. Banks and other institutions provide warnings and notifications of new discovered methods, and industry articles are written about this topic. It's important that the team keep abreast of new information and share it across the company.

Internal risks

Internal controls are more than only ensuring that no one steals from the company. It's also about the right processes, ensuring the numbers that are reported on are accurate and no stone is left unturned.

Internal risks can be due to human error, which is more likely than not, but you could also have someone acting fraudulently within the company. In my twenty-year career so far, I have encountered five examples of internal fraud. Two instances were staff managing to steal cash. One of these was petty cash theft, which isn't as relevant these days, and the other involved fraudulent expense claims. There was also an instance of an employee stealing a large amount of inventory.

Another instance was a huge learning curve for me. It was while I was working for a large corporation, and I had been newly promoted to the position of financial controller. One person in my team was tasked with reconciling all the transactions within the company. This was a full-time role, as automations weren't as sophisticated as they are today. Unfortunately, when I took over my new role, there were quite a few unreconciled accounts, and my mistake was to assume that my team were on it. They weren't.

An internal employee had managed to steal $20,000 over the course of six months. This should have been picked up much earlier, as then the internal employee would have been able to steal significantly less. This highlights an important lesson – always ensure that variances (particularly cash ones) are followed up immediately until resolved.

CASE STUDY: Misplaced trust

The final fraudulent activity I have encountered was with one of my clients. This company had grown so fast in the early years that their internal processes hadn't caught up with them. In fact, processes were pretty much ignored. The focus was on growth, which they achieved; tech, ensuring that the systems could handle the growth; and operations, ensuring supply could meet demand. Perfect for a growing startup.

Unfortunately, with outsourced bookkeepers, who were also struggling under the weight of volume, a few controls either never existed or were ignored. In this instance it was a bit of both.

I was brought into the company because the finances were in chaos. The founders didn't know their numbers, and any reports just didn't make sense. The board was frustrated, and they needed to tighten up their processes.

This was a tough job. It is an instance where the mantra from Chapter 3 – *under-promise and overperform* – was crucial. There were plenty of examples at this company where lax internal controls (pushing material numbers through the P&L) hindered the business, but most shocking to the founders was that one of their trusted team members was stealing from them.

As the bookkeeper was just trying to get reporting out, including VAT returns, they turned a blind eye to missing receipts and invoices. They did chase for these documents, but after a while it was all too hard. There was also no internal policy to fall back on.

The team member in question took advantage of that fact and started to submit fraudulent returns. After a few months, these returns started to become material, meaning my team picked up on the issue during the due diligence. These missing documents – a significant number, over time – were raised with the CEO, and it all collapsed into a heap within twenty-four hours.

This was a small team that had been working together for a while. They all trusted each other and had a great relationship – a typical startup culture. Unfortunately, this fraudster breached that trust, and it took a lot out of the team.

Even with a small team, always ensure that there are policies and procedures in place, and that they are adhered to.

Separation of duties in a startup

This can be a little bit tricky with small businesses. An ideal separation of duty process is when the individual who is approving payments is different to the person who reconciles the bank account, who is again different to the person who is preparing the payment. A lot of small businesses don't have three people working in finance, so it can be a challenge.

Taking the ideal situation, how can this be applied to a small business? With a small team, and in some cases it's only you, there's only so much that you can do here.

The first step is to consider using other members of the organisation. For example, the office manager or executive assistant may be able to do invoicing, if it isn't already outsourced. Another option is the head of operations or COO, who might be able to do a lot of approvals, along with the CEO or the founders. If there is an HR manager, they should be able to help with approving payroll.

Focus on the high-risk parts of the business, and with the transfer of cash and payroll, try and have as much separation of duties as possible.

Checks and accuracy

Have you ever sent the founder or an executive a piece of analysis, with a clear trend or finding, only to realise (or worse, to be told by the founder) that there is an error in the workings?

I have.

This is embarrassing, and the recipient will lose faith and trust in your abilities if it happens more than once. If finance is to be the source of truth and only have one set of numbers, checks and accuracy are essential.

"Next time be more careful where you put the decimal point!"

Human error

To mitigate this, all reporting needs what I like to call *checkers*. You need to introduce a formula that ensures checks are made independently from all the other inputs. You also want to take a step back and have a look at the report that's been produced. Ask yourself if the numbers make sense. At a high level, is the report reasonable? Sometimes, especially with budgeting, it helps to create charts from numbers to see the trends.

Revenue and expense recognition

In my experience, revenue and expense recognition is the first thing an auditor will check, along with purchasing policies. It's also a good idea to have a conversation with the founder and the leadership team about your recognition definitions (or proposed changes) so everyone is on the same page, especially if you believe it should change.

CASE STUDY: The founder's not always right

I once started working for a new startup, where the founder had a strong view on how revenue should be recognised and encouraged the bookkeeper to do the same, even though the founder's method was technically incorrect.

This caused quite an issue during their first big fundraising round when I first started with them. The savvy VCs quite rightly questioned this recognition policy, and the fundraise was heavily delayed while we were brought in to fix this and spend time restating all the historical revenue.

It's a good idea to get ahead of the game and have revenue and expense recognition sorted upfront, as it isn't always straightforward.

According to IFRS 15, revenue recognition is a five-step process:

1. Identify the contract.
2. Identify the performance obligation within the contract.
3. Determine the transaction price.

4. Allocate the transaction price.
5. Recognise the revenue when the obligation has been completed.

In general, the trickiest part of this is the fifth point, when the entity has completed the obligation. This is where founders can make mistakes. For example, if a customer purchases a product, and the delivery is in a week's time, the revenue cannot be recognised until the customer has received their goods.

Another challenge I have seen with revenue recognition amongst startups is that the bookkeeping team recognise revenue when the cash hits the bank account instead of when the cash is taken from the customer.

CASE STUDY: A coherent story

I worked with a startup where half of their revenue came via an affiliate network. Their original bookkeepers recognised the revenue when the affiliate network paid the startup. This caused a lot of issues with their KPIs, as they didn't match the revenue, as the revenue was lagging behind.

We then needed to communicate carefully with the board and investors on the change of revenue recognition decision. We also needed to recalculate what revenue would have looked like if it was done properly.

The expense recognition pillars principle, or matching principle, states that expenses should be recognised in the same period as the revenues they relate to. If not, expenses will likely be recognised as incurred, which might predate the period in which the related amount of the revenue is recognised.

Using the examples above, the cost of goods for the delivery of the product to the customer and the shipping costs would be in the same month as the revenue, ie either in the current month or deferred until the following month.

In a SaaS example, the most obvious cost of sale is the payment processing platform, such as Stripe, and generally the startup will receive an amount net of these fees. Either the cost is accrued in the month in which the cash isn't received, or it is recognised when the cash is received.

I also recommend creating a policy early on, once these recognition decisions have been made, communicated and confirmed. I have included a policy template in the book resources: www.financialleadershipfoundations.com/bookresources.

Purchasing policies

Outside of payroll, procurement or purchasing is the financial operations task that most of the company will interact with. Having a purchasing policy is therefore imperative so the business knows what to do and best practices are in place.

During a due diligence, I have seen many versions of bad practices that in general have been formed organically because there is no process. Everyone simply does what they think best or what they did in their previous workplace. Thankfully, many parts of this function are now automated, but initially there needs to be human interaction and decision making.

Another area to consider when looking for a new supplier or new service is the procurement process. I have uploaded a templated purchasing policy to our book resources: www.financialleadershipfoundations.com/bookresources. This highlights all considerations, from procurement to the final payment (P2P).

Risk management

There are many financial risks within a business, and it is the responsibility of the CFO to manage them. Some of the risks we have already touched on, but below are common risks that may need focus from finance leaders:

- **Liquidity risk:** This is the most common risk amongst startups and scaleups, as the businesses are generally loss making and rely on equity or debt fundraising. Chapter 7 covers cash management.

- **Debt risk:** This is still common amongst startups and scaleups, as not all businesses rely on equity fundraising alone. Many debt instruments include covenants, so the finance leader needs to ensure these aren't breached.
- **Compliance risk:** As mentioned in Chapter 5, ensure that all filings (financial statements, tax returns, etc) are completed accurately and on time and are the responsibility of the finance leader. For regulated FinTech businesses, it's important to ensure that both finance and operations follow the rules.
- **Process and operational risk:** Although not directly involved, a CFO can be involved in managing and mitigating these risks alongside the leadership team member responsible.
- **Personnel risk:** There is a great number of risks around the team, especially if the business decides to take drastic action, such as a redundancy round, which has been relatively common over the last two years. A CFO will be involved in this process.
- **Supply chain and key supplier risks:** Understanding the key suppliers and where the risks lie is key for the leadership team, and the CFO will often drive these conversations. Ideally, these risks are not only identified

but also mitigated – a breakdown with key suppliers can be devastating to the business.

- **Security and cyber risks:** These are well known, and the CFO will often need to negotiate an insurance policy to cover some of this risk, working with the CTO to ensure that the company has mitigated against it as much as possible. It's better to stop the cyber risk before it happens than to hope for an insurance payout after a huge cyber breach.
- **External and macro risks:** Of course, there are risks that are out of the control of the business (Brexit and Covid, for example), so the best course of action is a business continuity plan. Having this planned out and reviewed annually will ensure that if any large event happens – or even just roadworks around the office for a couple of days – the company's operations won't grind to a halt.

Summary

We've talked in this chapter about introducing internal and external controls, revenue recognition and introducing a few high-level policies as well as a risk management framework.

Actions for you:

- Review your internal controls and ensure they're fit for the purpose. Implement additional controls if there are any gaps.
- Implement an external supplier control (including change of bank details) immediately if this isn't in place.
- Review current separation of duties – are they suitable?
- All reports that leave the finance department should have checks in place and a high-level review before being sent.
- Implement a revenue recognition and purchasing policy if you haven't already. Again, templates are available in our book resources: www.financialleadershipfoundations.com/bookresources.
- Discuss risk management with the founder and leadership team and agree on the next steps.
- Consider which other policies and procedures are relevant to your company, and schedule in time to create and implement them.

7
All Things Cash

According to *The Telegraph*, 20% of new businesses fail in the first year and 60% fail in the first three years (May, 2019). Cashflow is one of the main reasons for these high statistics.

Cash is king

When considering the above statistic of new businesses failing, and the fact that this book is about leading the finance department for a startup and scaleup, cashflow is clearly one of the key responsibilities of a CFO.

A catchy saying, often attributed to an Australian business guru, goes like this: 'Turnover is vanity, profit is sanity, but cash is king.' If a business runs out of cash, that's it – the end. Isn't it?

When I first started working with startups, I was amazed at the tenacity of founders who just kept going and would always find another pocket of cash somewhere. Often this would pay off, but not always. Unfortunately, a startup where I worked for only two months went into receivership because they expanded too quickly before Covid, took debts to keep themselves afloat during the pandemic, and then found out there were no further last-minute pockets.

A CFO cannot rely on a founder to find pockets of cash. It's up to you, as the CFO, to always manage cash closely.

Cash management

Working with early-stage startups that are generally pre-Series A (see Chapter 12), cash is the number-one topic that I discuss with founders and sometimes the board.

I have found they're most interested in two KPIs:

1. Cash burn
2. Cash runway

I must stress that if a business isn't generating cash, it must be your top priority too!

1. Cash burn

This is all the incoming cash less all the outgoing cash for a given period – generally a month. The cash burn number will always be at the bottom of the cashflow statement. However, I do always exclude any equity injections or debt drawdowns to see the true cash burn number. I also look at cash burn on a rolling three-month basis as many expenses are paid quarterly (rent and VAT/GST, for example).

2. Cash runway

This is simply how many months the company has left before it runs out of cash.

In a stable business that isn't pivoting regularly, relying on fundraising and growing more than 10% year over year, calculating cash runway by using cash burn works nicely. However, this is not the case with a startup or scaleup. This is largely due to the business's cash burn changing month to month and most certainly from one quarter to the next. Cash spent today is often not going to help you estimate the business's cash burn in six months' time.

Most startups' cash burn will increase over time until it comes to a point of moving towards profitability. If you are using the cash burn number to calculate runway, you can run the risk of either overestimating or underestimating the business's cash runway, which can have dire consequences.

Imagine informing a founder that they have eighteen months' cash runway, when it's actually more like eight months. You may soon be looking for another job.

Ideally, a founder (and board) would want to have twelve to eighteen months' cash runway when going into a fundraise. It doesn't always happen, of course – I've certainly seen less than that – however, founders need a bit of time to prepare, so the longer the cash runway, the better. If it's less than twelve months, the founder should already be speaking to potential investors.

How to calculate cash runway if you can't rely on cash burn

For a startup and scaleup, you calculate the business's cash runway by using the live forecast. I cover budgeting and forecasting in Chapter 11, but I want to highlight here the concept of a rolling forecast. For a startup or scaleup that is pivoting and changing directions, the main reason a rolling forecast is necessary is so that you can manage the business's cash runway.

Working capital

Calculating the business's working capital is straightforward – it's simply current assets minus current liabilities. Working capital represents the net resources available to finance day-to-day operations. If the business has negative working capital, it will have liquidity issues.

Ideally, a business that has a positive cash conversion cycle (CCC), ie where cash from customers is received before having to pay suppliers, is less likely to run out of cash and over time will need to rely less on fund-raising to stay afloat. However, the opposite is also true. It's worthwhile establishing this cycle within the business model to ensure that the business stays afloat and doesn't run out of cash or have constant cashflow issues.

When looking at your working capital, make sure you look at the details, particularly when needing to extend the cash runway. The aim is to increase the speed of inflows and decrease the speed of outflows by improving the CCC. Obviously, the business needs to increase its revenue in general and can also cut costs, but ignoring working capital and CCC won't help cashflows. How do you improve working capital with existing revenues and costs? It's all about timing.

Here are a few ways that you can increase the inflows:

- **Issue invoices quickly and ensure they go to the right person.** This may sound obvious, but I have seen the opposite being an issue more than once.
- **Shorten credit terms.** Instead of allowing a 45-day payment term, can you negotiate it down? How about upfront payment, particularly if you have project-based or subscription-based products or services?
- **Incentivise early payments.** Offer small discounts for customers who pay their invoices early.

Here are a few ways that you can decrease the outflows:

- **Negotiate with suppliers.** Can you extend payment terms with your vendors or negotiate bulk discounts? If relevant, work with credit insurers to increase your terms.
- **Review inventory levels.** Overstocking ties up cash. Regularly review inventory levels to ensure you're not over-purchasing.
- **Automate payments but with caution.** While automating can ensure you never miss a payment, schedule them closer to due dates to retain cash longer.

- **Consider credit cards instead of debit cards.** Although debit cards offer lots of benefits, you are paying for goods with zero-day terms. If you can pay for these via a credit card that offers 45-day terms, you'll have 45-day terms with these suppliers. Just ensure that the credit card annual fee isn't too high.

Raising equity

If you have worked for a startup or scaleup for a while, this is a familiar concept. If you haven't: raising equity is a process of selling shares in the company for cash, either immediately or in the future.

As these businesses aren't listed on any stock exchange, this process is direct. Founders speak to investors about their business and hopefully sell some of their company shares to investors who are interested in their business. Think *Dragons' Den* or *Shark Tank*; raising equity is less intense but possibly just as stressful. In general, startups and scaleups rely on this type of fundraising to grow the business and eventually turn a profit. Fundraising (raising equity) comes at different stages of the business and attracts different types of investors.

At the early stage of a business, where the business is just a concept, and founders still need to get product–market fit (PMF) before they can scale, the focus of the business is to have the product or service up and running and achieve PMF. To achieve PMF, there can be many different iterations of the product or service, and leaders need to ensure there is enough customer demand.

A lot of preparation and many discussions go nowhere, and the PMF process can be quick or can take years. At the time of writing, I'm working for a startup that has just entered its second year, and we are on product iteration number three as there wasn't enough demand with the first two.

Once PMF is achieved and the acquisition channel is working efficiently, the later funding rounds are largely to fund the growth – in general to invest in sales and marketing, tech, and product development or expansion.

Investors will invest in a business that they believe will be valued at ten times its current worth – or much more – in the future. That period used to be up to ten years, but the time frame is getting shorter. This has a lot to do with many tech-based businesses that are growing rapidly in the fast-growth industry.

Angels, private equity (PE) firms and venture capitalists (VCs) will help grow businesses via investment. However, certain investors will provide guidance and advice to help the business flourish. Investors often form part of the board and give the founders guidance and mentoring, as they've often had a lot of experience of growing businesses. Investors also often have an extensive network that founders will be able to tap into.

When debt should be a consideration

There are many instances when debt should be considered as an alternative to equity. Below you'll find pros and cons of each as direct comparisons.

There are pros with raising debt, and it should be considered as an option when comparing all alternatives and thinking about future cashflow.

Early-stage startups may consider asset finance to purchase equipment, or revenue for stock investment, to help manage working capital. Later-stage scaleups may consider larger loans to help boost growth and protect the dilution of ownership; and large asset investments, which are better suited to debt.

Short-term debt

The most common short-term debt that most business already have are the business's supplier terms and credit cards. Another quick short-term debt that may be worth considering is a bank overdraft. This depends on the relationship the business has with the bank, and the type of bank the business uses.

Other options are director loans, or short-term loans from existing investors. As an example: there may be a 30-day situation, where the business might be struggling to pay payroll while awaiting revenue to come in, particularly in the very early days, and the director may settle the payroll. Then the business can pay the director back, perhaps a month or two later.

When I worked for Funding Circle in 2012, there were not many short-term debt options for small businesses. Large banks were the primary providers, and the founders of Funding Circle saw a gap here and created a company to fill that gap. However, there are now many more short-term debt options. The only caveat I would highlight here is that many unsecured short-term loans are secured with a personal guarantee (PG). PGs usually ask the founder and director to personally guarantee the loan, which means that if the business finds it cannot repay the loan for whatever reason, the founder must pay the loan back. This is high risk for the founder personally, and in general, I would not recommend it. However, the decision is up to the founder, the board and their lawyer.

Long-term debt

Going to a bank and asking for a three-year loan thankfully isn't the only option for startups and scaleups. I say thankfully because banks will generally only grant larger loans for businesses who are making profit. As most startups and scaleups are not profitable, this is not an option. However, there are some banks (and other institutions) that do offer venture debt, and this may be a consideration if the business has raised a good amount of equity from a venture capitalist.

Venture debt extends the runway of the business, without further diluting the existing shareholders' equity stake, by relying on the venture capitalist's due diligence and knowledge in the industry. This allows the business to borrow a sizeable amount, normally over a three-year term. Some venture debt providers want the business to be profitable towards the end of the term of the loan, and there are often warrants associated with this instrument. However, if the business has just raised a Series B+ with a well-known VC, this is an option and worth considering.

Asset, revenue, inventory and invoice finance are other forms of longer-term debt that provide options for loss-making startups and scaleups, and these provide a secured form of debt.

Debt vs equity

Raising equity is the most common form of fundraising for fast-growth businesses as there is no interest to pay or obligation to repay investors. However, there are cons with this method as well and so, when needing extra cash to extend the runway, debt should also be considered as an option.

What are the pros and cons of each alternative? Let's start with equity.

Pros of equity investment include:

- Equity fundraising doesn't need to be repaid directly to investors.
- Certain types of investors such as angels and VCs often provide valuable guidance, mentorship and access to networks, alongside their investment.
- The interest in the business's future is usually aligned with the founder and investors, which isn't always the case with a lender.

Cons with equity investment include:

- For founders, this is a big one to consider. Raising equity fundraising means sharing control and diluting the cap table (or capitalisation table).

Should the business grow as planned or an exit is looking likely, the cost of dilution could be much higher than the cost of interest repayments. It is worth doing a proper analysis; in some situations, you may be surprised at the difference.

- With new investors come varied opinions and perspectives, which can complicate decision-making processes. Ideally, you want to keep your board as lean as possible.
- Raising capital can take many months, and it will generally take up nearly all of the founder's time. Consider who can take on their role during this time.

As a comparison, the pros of raising debt are:

- You're borrowing capital, which means you retain full control.
- Loans have repayment schedules, which allow for more precise financial forecasting and predictability.
- When the debt is completely paid, there is in general no further liability (some venture debt deals include warrants).
- Smaller loans can be raised in a matter of days or a few weeks.

Cons with debt instruments include:

- Loans are a liability, and the business must repay the loan with interest. There may also be obligations other than just the repayments. A good example is covenants; you may find that a lender will want certain covenants to cover some level of risk. These obligations may restrict the business's flexibility.
- For early-stage startups, qualifying for a loan can be difficult without collateral or a strong financial history. PGs are also common requirements of small business loans. Founders should be careful when assessing these kinds of loans and should consider seeking legal advice.
- Business or personal assets (in the case of a PG) are at risk if a loan isn't repaid.

The decision between equity and debt financing is different for every business, and the ideal solution depends on the business's life cycle, its financial projections, the founder's and investors' willingness to share control, and their tolerance for risk.

Summary

We've talked here about cash runway, cash burn and working capital. I've also introduced raising debt, raising equity, and comparing the two.

Actions for you:

- Ensure that your cash burn, cash runway and any other cashflow metrics are included in your monthly reporting.
- Review your current inflows and see if there is a way to improve the timing.
- Review your current outflows and see if you need to improve the terms or other methods.
- Include weekly cashflow reporting as part of your reviews.
- With longer-term cashflow, consider the different equity and debt options for your company.
- Chat to your founder about their appetite for debt. However, be mindful that not all founders understand the pros and cons, so an exploratory discussion may be worthwhile.

PART THREE
MONITORING AND REPORTING

This is the third part of the Financial Leadership Fundamentals Framework. After the baseline is accurate, the next step is to upgrade the reporting. What is a leader's role in the management accounts? How can the reporting be interesting and start conversations? The next two chapters will cover software considerations as well as how to upgrade the reporting.

8 The Leader's Role In Monthly Reporting

Monthly management accounts may seem like an odd topic to include in a book for future finance leaders, especially if you may have churned out tens if not hundreds of management accounts so far in your career.

That's the point, though. Sometimes you and your team may do this task on autopilot. Sometimes you may rush through the reviews just so you can start your holiday – no one understands scheduling holidays at the ends of months like a management accountant. Sometimes you only think about the management accounts on the first business day of the month (or the fifth, when it's time for you to check in with the team).

However, the management accounts are the *only* piece of work that you and your team do that is seen by the most senior people in the business… *every single month.* It is sent to the founder/CEO, the leadership team and the board. It's also sent to investors and potential investors, and to your bank, lenders, auditors, etc.

When you think about the list of people monthly management accounts go to, it makes sense that your best work needs to go into this. A finance leader cannot be great if the management accounts are subpar.

Once upon a time, I churned out the management accounts without too much thought as I was too busy with other things. It takes time to upgrade and put thought into the reporting. I've worked with some clients who started with a low base, and it took months to get it to a good place. However, once the management accounts are interesting to read, show different analysis each month and add value to the business, leaders around the business reach out to you more frequently. Not only are you asked to do more analysis, but your point of view is also invited. You get a seat at the decision-making table.

Management accounts are so important that I offer a mini course on this exact topic, and this whole chapter is dedicated to it too.

Preparation

Preparation is key when upgrading the reporting. Most of the work here was covered in the prior chapters (see Part Two), but there are still a few further tasks.

The first is the structure of the P&L. Is the P&L structure similar to the default structure of the general ledger, with a few extra account codes thrown in? Or is the structure of the P&L well thought out, with subtotals and revenue categories that align with the commercials of the business? Have you had a discussion with the founders about how they talk about the business model and how the business makes money, and does your P&L structure reflect the same story?

Look at the structure and challenge yourself on whether this is the right fit, especially if this review hasn't been done before, or if the business has pivoted slightly and the P&L hasn't changed.

How to make reporting interesting

There are a few ways to make reporting more interesting. The first one is commentary, which I'll cover below, under the heading 'The 5 Whys'.

The next is to include more than just three financial statements. As the management accounts are sent to non-accountants, some of your audience may not be able to read numbers like we do. Instead, they'll glaze over the numbers and get bored, or worse still not even read the report. Include clear and concise charts that highlight your key points. Pictures tell a thousand words.

Another way to make reporting more interesting is to change it up. If you show the same three financial statements plus the same two charts every single month, with no real thought of insight given, the report gets boring. Instead, consider adding in something new each month. What have you and your team discovered? What trend is giving you concern? What product has the best profitability and needs focus to grow further? What are the next steps of the business, considering the results?

If you add in different charts, graphs and aspects such as trend analysis, the management team will look forward to what you have to say each month rather than opening the management accounts file only because they feel they must.

The 5 Whys

This method is so effective at producing interesting commentary that I encourage everyone in my team to use it every month.

Essentially, your commentary should add more than what the numbers demonstrate. If the commentary could be created by anyone who reads the numbers, it's not adding anything interesting to the report.

Here's how the 5 Whys system works: keep asking yourself *Why?* until you get to the root cause of a variance. You may only need to ask *Why?* three or four times, but often it will be five times.

Here is an example:

'Revenue is £50K less than last month and £10K less than budget.' *Who cares! This can be read from the report. Why?*

'The subscriber number dropped and there was high churn.' *This can be read from the KPIs. Why?*

'Some subscribers stopped using the service due to technical issues.' *OK, better – but why?*

'A key supplier isn't hitting their SLAs, which is affecting our ability to serve, and we need to find a replacement supplier.' *There you go!*

Determining the right KPIs

Dr William Edwards Deming, an influential American statistician, reportedly made the astute comment,

'Without data, you're just another person with an opinion.'

Here are just some of the benefits of KPIs:

- **Insight.** KPIs often tell a more compelling story than the financial statements on their own, and they can give great insight into the financials. As KPIs can demonstrate performance, they can give a reason to the *Why?* question.
- **Analysis.** KPIs also help you to analyse the longer-term performance of the business. A startup or scaleup's year-on-year financials may look very different, as there may be 100% growth, additional product lines or a much bigger team. A KPI can demonstrate overall performance and volume, particularly regarding sales and marketing funnels and operational performance.
- **Benchmarking.** KPIs are useful in comparing the business with other businesses within the same industry. Even if the other business is ten times the size of yours, by focusing on the available KPIs you can see how the performance differs.

As a starting point, I always look at the definition of each KPI and compare it across the business. There is no point in adding KPIs to the monthly reports if the definition and therefore results of the KPIs differ to those of other departments. The board reporting should have one version of the truth throughout, not different customer numbers depending on who completes the slides.

The next step is to look at the strategic (long-term) goals. In general, these will form the North Star KPI – the one that measures your company's core value and success. For example, the business may have a big customer number goal, a gross merchandising value (GMV) goal or a subscription goal that it wants to reach over the coming years. This should be the main KPI that is reported on.

Each department will have many metrics. The trick is to work out which metrics are important and worth reporting on as KPIs. Again, start that with the end goals. Work with the leadership team on what should be reported on each month, based on their operational goals for the quarter and for longer term. Keep the list short and to the point.

This isn't to say that the other metrics won't be measured. The challenge is to work out what tells the story of the team's aspirations without being bogged down with hundreds of metrics.

To keep the management accounts interesting, spotlight KPIs when trends change or there is something worth highlighting. Working out what the right KPIs are for any business is a never-ending process. Always challenge yourself and the business on adding KPIs to (or subtracting them from) the reporting, especially if goals, products or services change.

Fundraising and unit economics

Ultimately, investors want to invest in a business that is growing and will continue growing exponentially without wasting lots of capital, resulting in a higher valuation in a few years' time. Since 2022, when the fundraising market slowed, European investors have also been keen to ensure that a business isn't too risky and will ultimately break even and turn profitable in the near future.

Keeping these motivations in mind, the KPIs that the business will need to demonstrate are:

- **How quickly your company can grow with extra capital:** Growth and costs to grow KPIs are important as well as how much revenue the business will get back from these customers.
- **ROI:** Investors will also want to know how quickly the business can break even and return a profit. These KPIs needs to indicate the drivers to reach this goal and the worst-case scenario – *what does the business look like if the goals aren't reached?* – so decisions can be made today.
- **Environmental and social impact metrics:** These metrics are becoming more common and will be

required for all future fundraising. Include these in your list going forward.

I have found that the following KPIs tend to be relatively important to all businesses. These KPIs will be required for both actual and forecasted:

- YoY (year-over-year) revenue growth (ARR, or Annual Returning Revenue, if relevant)
- Total number of active/paying customers
- Repeat customers and NPS (net promoter score) or other customer satisfaction metrics
- CAC (cost of acquisition), LTV (lifetime value) and payback period
- Churn
- Gross, contribution and profit margins
- Cash runway, cash burn, burn multiple and cash balance
- Headcount
- Road to breakeven
- Market leadership metrics
- Environmental and social impact KPIs (for example, net results metrics, inclusion and diversity metrics)
- Unit economics

A few industry-specific KPIs will also need to be added.

See more details on the above KPIs at www.financial-leadershipfoundations.com/bookresources.

Board and investor reporting

Before coming to month end, it is (unsurprisingly!) worth doing some preparation for the board. First steps include:

1. **Looking at the latest shareholders' agreement:** This will include the minimum reporting requirements. It is your role to ensure that there is no breach of contractual obligations and therefore, ensure that any Board and Investor reporting includes these obligations as a minimum.
2. **Establishing how much information the board wants or needs:** This can be achieved via a frank discussion with the founder/CEO. Sometimes the founder has a strong relationship with the board and leans on them heavily for advice and therefore wants more details to be communicated. This isn't always the case, but it's good to get a steer from the founder/CEO on how much information – over and above the summarised financial statements – is required.

Here are some tips for creating a board deck:

- Include charts and graphs. Like the management accounts, these help to get the message across.
- Use bullet points instead of long paragraphs.
- Ensure that the financial statements are summarised and easy to read and understand.
- Always include comparisons – compare the results to prior periods, budget and competitors. The board need context.
- Include forward-looking statements – what's next? What are the business predictions?

A good board report for a startup or scaleup should be concise yet comprehensive. Here's a suggested structure that can be used as a starting point and developed for your business:

1. **Executive summary:** Begin with a clear, brief overview of the company's performance and key financials for the period. This will provide the board with a snapshot of the company's status.
2. **Traffic lights:** Show clearly what worked well (green), what is in limbo or work in progress (amber) and what hasn't worked well (red). This is more specific than the overall summary.
3. **Progress:** Depending on the life cycle of the business, include either the product development

and key milestones here or jump straight into the financials.

4. **Income statement:** Give a summary, highlighting revenue streams, profit margins and significant expenses. Use this section to provide context to the numbers, explaining any variances or unusual items. Highlight accomplishments and challenges achieved in the period.

5. **Balance sheet:** Include a summary with comparisons with the prior year, month and budget. Highlight important changes and what they mean for the company's financial health.

6. **Cashflow statement:** Along with the summarised statement, explain the changes and variances. Also useful here are cash runway, cash burn and road to breakeven.

7. **Financial ratios and KPIs:** Include relevant financial ratios and KPIs that give insights into the performance of the business and help to tell the story that the business wants to convey to the board. It is good to use charts and graphs here rather than only lots of numbers.

8. **Progress update towards business goals:** Discuss the progress in strategic goals, operational milestones, and any market or product expansion plans.

9. **Risk management and opportunities:** This section should offer both potential risks and mitigation plans as well as potential opportunities.
10. **Special focus areas:** Depending on the current business cycle or specific challenges, include sections on fundraising, market analysis or capital expenditure. Sometimes the board will request a certain topic to be addressed or a closer look of an aspect of the business, which can be presented here. On occasion, this section can take up most of the board discussions.
11. **Conclusion and recommendations:** End with actionable insights and recommendations.

Summary

We've talked in this chapter about how to prepare for monthly reporting, and how to make management accounts interesting through storytelling, KPIs and charts. We've also discussed the importance of KPIs, and what and how to report to investors and to the board.

Actions for you:

- Revisit your P&L structure and ensure that it is fit for purpose. Is this how the founder sees the business? Any changes, ensure the P&L changes with it.

- Constantly review the management accounts to ensure that they are adding value.
- If the most important KPIs haven't yet been identified, work out with the founder what should always be reported externally and to the board. Ensure the KPIs are aligned with the goals of the business.
- Check for KPI definitions and one version of the truth.
- Challenge what broader KPIs should be included in the monthly reporting.
- Consider spotlighting a different trend each month.
- Spend time working out the unit economics and LTV for the business.
- Compare the KPIs with those of others in the industry or of similar businesses.
- Check the shareholders' agreement to ensure all reporting requirements are met.
- Have a discussion with the founder/CEO regarding how and what they want to communicate to the board.

9

Processes And The Finance Tech Stack

It's no secret that there have been enormous advancements in technology over the years. Within finance it's been prevalent in the last five years, and this will no doubt continue in the next five years to come.

It doesn't feel too long ago that I had an accounts payable clerk, two bank reconciliation clerks and an accounts receivable clerk, though maybe I'm just showing my age! Increased automation due to technological advances of course reduces the need for some financial roles.

One challenge for smaller businesses is the cost of the tech. Thankfully, there are inexpensive yet powerful options, but there is still quite a way to go, particularly with budgeting.

I update my website every six months, including the current finance tech stack I'm using with startups and scaleups. Here's a link to that information: www.financialleadershipfoundations.com/bookresources.

What is a finance tech stack?

A finance tech stack is a set of software and tools to manage the day-to-day operations. The components of a finance tech stack may vary depending on the size, budget and complexity of the business.

Below are the different options you can consider when building or upgrading your finance tech stack:

- **Accounting software:** The general ledger is the most obvious of any finance tech stack. No doubt your business has a general ledger. The challenge is when to upgrade your software, which we'll discuss below with ERPs.
- **Budgeting and forecasting tools:** There are a few competitors in this field. I haven't yet found one that has created perfect tools and am looking forward to that. If your business has a larger budget (in excess of USD1,000 per month), you have a few options. See my latest recommendations at www.financialleadershipfoundations.com/bookresources.

- **Financial reporting software:** This software allows businesses to create and share financial reports, including balance sheets, income statements and cashflow statements. They also help with consolidation (thank heavens!), management accounts, overhead reporting and board reporting. This is one area where software has improved enormously and has shaved hours of time off financial reporting at month end.
- **Financial operations software:** This area has also exploded, and there are many tasks that can be automated and just as many options. To name a few, there are payment processing software options as well as invoicing software, both in the receipt and data input of invoices as well as for producing invoices. There is also payroll software for automating the payment of employees and calculated taxes.
- **Business intelligence (BI) tools:** These allow businesses to analyse and visualise financial data to identify trends and make data-driven decisions. These are brilliant if they are implemented well and have a strong data/BI team to support them.
- **Equity management software:** This software helps businesses manage the cap table by keeping track of all the investments or grants and the necessary reporting required.

- **CRM software:** This helps businesses manage customer interactions and track customer data. This software generally sits with the marketing/ sales team, but the finance team often will interact with this tool.

Not every business needs a complex and comprehensive finance tech stack. For small businesses or early-stage startups with basic accounting needs, a simpler tech stack may be more appropriate.

When building a finance tech stack, here are some of the most important things to consider when selecting finance software and tools:

- **Cost:** Some finance software and tools can be expensive, so it is important to select tools that fit within the business's budget. It's also worth considering the total cost of all the tools, especially for smaller businesses. Most finance tech stacks include multiple tools that plug into the general ledger. Each individual tool may not be overly costly on its own, but implementing multiple tools can get expensive.
- **Integration:** It is important to select software and tools that integrate with each other to avoid duplication of effort and to ensure that data is easily accessible across systems.
- **Scalability:** This is particularly important for fast-growth businesses. As your business grows,

your finance tech stack needs may change. It is important to select tools that can scale with your business needs.

- **Security:** This is an important consideration for your risk register. Financial data is sensitive, so it is important to select software and tools that have strong security features and protect against data breaches.
- **User-friendliness:** This is also an important factor – the software should be easy to manage so your team can use it effectively.
- **Time:** Implementing a new piece of kit can be time-consuming. Ensure you have the right resources available and try to schedule most of the heavy lifting around month end.

What should be done first?

While software can be great for improving the accuracy and efficiency within financial operations, it's important to remember that software alone cannot fix issues with inaccurate data or bad processes.

Before implementing any new software, it's important to ensure that your financial processes and numbers are accurate and reliable. It can be tempting to rely on software to catch errors or provide a quick fix, but this will not help you, and the software implementation may fail. Instead, take the time to review and audit your financial processes and numbers, making any changes or corrections before implementing new software (see Part Two).

Once you have ensured that your financial processes and numbers are accurate and reliable, it will be time to consider moving away from Excel and Google Sheets and towards software that is more efficient and accurate. While Excel and Google Sheets are useful tools, they have limitations when it comes to managing complexity, and they are prone to human error. Although spreadsheets may be quick to set up, updating an old spreadsheet can be more time-consuming than introducing another software tool. Consolidation is a prime example here.

What is an ERP, and when is it time to upgrade?

ERP stands for *enterprise resource planning*. It's a software that takes all the different parts of your business – finance, supply chain, operations, reporting, manufacturing and human resources – and ties them all together in one resource. This might sound too good to be true, and sometimes it is. ERP systems are expensive and can takes a long time to implement (six to twelve months). At some point, however, a business needs a bigger system.

One of the most common questions I get when talking about the finance tech stack is when a business should upgrade from the simpler inexpensive general ledgers or accounting software such as Xero, QuickBooks and MYOB and move to an ERP.

How to know when it's time to level up

Here are some important factors in deciding when to move to a full-blown ERP system:

- If your customer details are in one system and financial data in another, ERPs are great for bringing everything together.
- ERPs can automate many manual tasks, so if there are too many inefficiencies, an ERP may be able to help.
- ERP systems include real-time tracking, which makes managing your inventory much simpler, including across multiple locations. I have worked with ERPs that had a good WMS (warehouse management system). This can be a real time saver, especially at month end and for any inventory analysis or product profitability analysis.
- If your accounting software is struggling to keep up with your business growth and can't deal with the volume of transactions, it's probably time for a change. With fast-growth businesses,

this is generally the most common reason businesses upgrade to an ERP.

- You may also find that scaling internationally, new regulation, introducing new products and services, or even a new business line will cause issues with your current accounting software. This is due to volume and complexity issues and also to the ability to segment the market and do matrix reporting.

Due to the sheer cost of an ERP and the six to twelve months it takes to integrate one (it is not light work, even if you have a third-party project management team), I recommend keeping a general ledger for as long as possible. However, going back to Chapter 5: if you don't have a good baseline, something needs to change. Upgrade your processes first and then perhaps your software.

Process improvement and SaaS

As the finance function has many internal reporting requirements and needs to complete KPI calculations, sometimes a bottleneck can form due to outdated or manual processes that consume excessive time and resources. It isn't uncommon for a finance leader to find they're spending too much time firefighting and that process improvements and automations are overlooked.

As mentioned in Chapter 1: book time in your calendar for thinking and planning. Ignoring this will only discourage the team and hinder any leadership skills, and the finance function will fall behind the rest of the business. You therefore need to make this a priority.

Automation

With automation, the issue and solution are not just about buying new software solutions – you need to review and restructure your processes to ensure they meet the business needs. This might include automating mundane tasks like bank reconciliations or accounts payable, and also rethinking the entire workflow to reduce manual touchpoints.

CASE STUDY: Streamlining credit control

One of our clients had a time-consuming credit control process. We found that the initial communication with their clients – sending out reminders and chasing payments – had been automated, using a SaaS tool we were familiar with. However, the stages before and after this, such as dispute resolution and final account settlements, were heavily manual and were taking the team many days a week to manage.

By focusing on these components, streamlining and automating, the company significantly reduced the time spent on credit control, from four days a week to mere hours.

Efficiency

One effective method to assess the efficiency of your processes is to implement a simple timesheet system for your team. It doesn't need to be overly complicated – a basic log of activities every hour for a couple of weeks can reveal significant insights into where time and effort are being spent and, more importantly, wasted.

When reviewing your processes, you may find areas that can be automated to improve efficiency. This isn't just about replacing manual tasks with software. It's about rethinking the entire process to make sure each part is necessary and fits into the entire workflow. Sometimes it's worth ignoring the existing process temporarily, coming up with a perfect process and then bridging the gaps.

I need to stress that process improvement isn't a one-time fix; it's a continuous process. If processes haven't been reviewed in a long time, tackle one area at a time and then go back and review them annually.

Data

Data doesn't always sit within the CFO's remit. It is used heavily by the finance function, though, and should therefore be front of mind and a topic of conversation with the leadership team. A data strategy has become a more important component for any startup or scaleup (and for any other business).

One of the first steps in building an effective data strategy is establishing one version of the truth. As discussed with KPIs in Chapter 8, it is essential to understand the definitions and ensure that the data reconciles so that there is just one number or result for each KPI.

As your startup grows, the need to transition to a better data strategy is important for the long-term success of the business. Here are a few points the business needs to consider when looking for that longer-term data strategy:

- Identify what data is essential for your business operations and decision making, and how this data is currently being captured, stored and used.
- Find a software that suits your business and is simple to use.
- Ensure the software is scalable for future growth.
- Establish clear policies and procedures for data entry, maintenance and access.
- Train your team on the importance of data integrity and how to use the new software effectively. If a new data reporting tool is implemented, ensure that the teams know how to pull the data properly. Otherwise, you will find

yourself with multiple versions of the truth, as different teams are pulling the same data slightly differently.

Using AI

With the introduction of ChatGPT in late 2022, AI is now part of our lives and no longer science fiction. My main takeaway for this part of the book is to encourage you to stay up to date with what new technologies are offering us. AI can be incredibly useful, and it is developing and improving rapidly. I want to include a starting point for AI, as I still encounter many accountants who don't use it at all.

- **Financial KPIs.** I have used AI to do quick financial analysis on much larger companies (when I'm looking at suppliers and competitors and completing other due diligence) rather than the startups that I work with. I have also dumped financial data into AI and asked it to come up with various financial metrics, which I pick and choose from, as a lot aren't necessarily relevant for smaller companies.
- **Internal communication.** I have used AI to help me with summarising large reports, board reports and financial summaries into shorter and less formal language. If I have written text that is long or clunky, I ask AI to rework it.

- **Executive summaries.** It is easy to dump the long-form report into AI and ask it to write an executive summary. This takes seconds, although you do need to proofread it before finalising.
- **Written policies.** I have built up internal policies using AI. I have found this works well by providing me with a framework or a base to start with, which I then edit to make the policies more suitable.
- **Excel formulas and tech code.** This is a no-brainer. AI is powerful in showing how to do Excel formulas or any other tech code.
- **Certain types of software.** AI helps with certain types of software such as PowerBI, SAP, etc. For example, if you don't know how to perform a function, you can ask AI and it will give you specific instructions for your query.
- **Titles, names and copy.** As a leader of a smaller company, you are often helping the leadership team with more than just numbers. Sometimes you will need to brainstorm names, catchphrases, sales copy or marketing, or even the name of a new product. This is where AI comes into its own.
- **Email templates.** For emails to board members, templates for your credit control or long emails to investors, without hesitation I ask AI to prepare the initial template and then edit it to suit my needs.

- **'How to' questions.** Anytime I have a question for a search engine, I'm now getting into the habit of asking AI first. For questions on legislation and the latest accounting standards, it still has a little way to go, but it continues to improve. There are AI tools that give you links to their sources of information, so I also then drill into the source. An example of when this hasn't worked is when I asked AI for current UK grants. It gave me a list of grants and (thankfully), the links to the sources. When following the links, I did find that a few were out of date, so be thorough here.

I'm sure there are a hundred different ways that CFOs can use this tool, and I'm keen to learn more. Please let me know of anything you have discovered, and I'll include your tips in the next finance tech stack update within our book resources.

Summary

This chapter has covered software improvement (and how to prepare for it), the finance tech stack, improving processes, what an ERP is and when to upgrade, and AI.

Actions for you:

- Make note of all workflows that are within the finance function or across the departments.
- Do a timesheet exercise regularly, in which you and your team make notes of what they do each hour over a couple of weeks.
- Review the timesheets and look for time-consuming tasks.
- Identify areas for process improvements and brainstorm ideal processes.
- Project plan the gaps and look for potential solutions.
- Review your finance tech stack to ensure good workflows and efficiencies.
- Plan for when an upgrade is necessary.
- Keep yourself educated on new tech and AI developments.

PART FOUR

ADDING VALUE

This is the fourth part of the Financial Leadership Fundamentals Framework. After the baseline is accurate and regular reporting has been upgraded, we can focus on adding value. This part focuses on business partnerships, budgeting, forecasting and, of course, preparing to fundraise.

10
Business Partnerships

I was introduced to the concept of business partnering while I was a finance director at Funding Circle. I was already conducting some elements of business partnering, but once I learned the benefits of partnering from the perspective of the business and of finance – and from my own perspective – I decided to step it up.

What is business partnering?

A statement on the ACCA Global website explains how finance business partners:

- Collaborate with other business departments
- Form partnerships with operations and management

- Assist executives by providing financial information, tools, analysis and insight
- Challenge executives' thinking, helping them make more informed decisions and driving business strategy
- Provide real-time support and analysis
- Add value to help with decision making

Essentially, this is the concept of forming partner relationships, which are usually a support function for a more operational department head. The goal is to encourage collaboration, which in turn improves business performance.

From a finance perspective, I see business partnering as a method to increase communication with the business and to add considerable value. It will also get you a seat at the decision-making table.

The chart below highlights the different levels of the finance function. Business partnering is strategic and sits in the bottom part of the chart – the high level. It's the area that finance professionals in leadership roles should partake in.

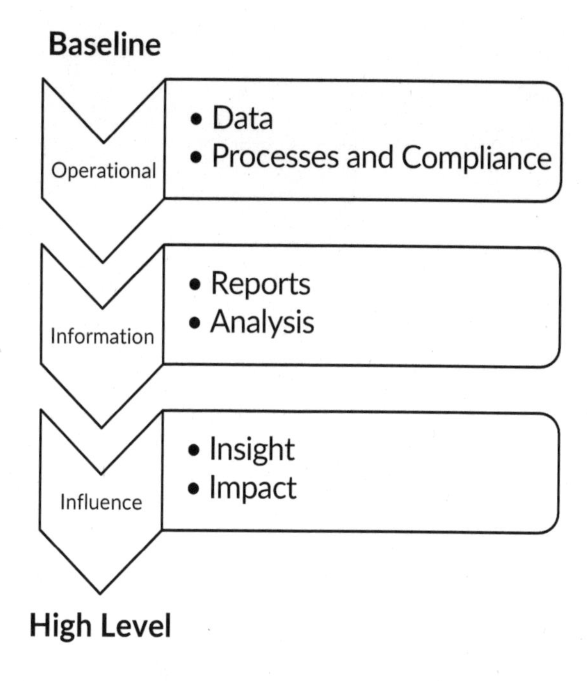

Different levels of value

The goal of this relationship for you is that you are part of the team and able to collaborate and communicate with other departments. For example, when the managers of the marketing team need to review a potential marketing channel, you are part of this discussion. You will work with the marketing team to assess this opportunity and whether it's worth testing or not.

Another example of successful business partnerships is when the finance leader and representative partners with the operations team work together to streamline supply chain processes. If the finance team can help identify potential cost savings and operational improvements, this will directly impact the operations team achieving their goals and, in turn, help the bottom line.

Benefits

Business partnering provides many benefits for you (as you develop your career and visibility), for the finance team, for the teams and leaders you're forming relationship with, and ultimately, for business performance.

How this helps you, as a new or aspiring leader

When working as a finance manager or financial controller, traditionally you spend most of your time working within the finance department. Any communication outside finance is then spent chasing documentation (invoices, receipts, etc), obtaining information regarding transactions, and confirming payroll information. The role is more about information and data gathering than collaboration and adding value.

As discussed in Chapters 1 and 3, the leadership role focuses more on relationships with other departments, working with the business and looking forward than on processing information and hitting deadlines. However, when you start in a new leadership role, relationships and opportunities to help solve problems and set goals and strategies aren't handed to you. You need to make them happen, and the best way is through business partnering.

A good finance leader doesn't work in solo and ignore the rest of the leadership team. Collaboration, strategic thinking and communication form a huge part of the role. The sooner business partnering is embraced and practised, the better leadership skills will be developed.

Strong business partnership relationships around the business are also beneficial for the finance function. Understanding what is going on around the business throughout the month prepares the finance team to understand what the numbers are trying to tell them. This is from both backward-looking and forward-looking perspectives. A finance leader should be looking at the historical numbers and working out how they can help with the future of the business. A true understanding of what is occurring throughout the business facilitates the practice of recommending next steps and future actions.

There is nothing better than receiving the first draft of the management accounts from the team and finding no surprises within the results. Instead, as the finance team is already aware of the goals achieved and the challenges incurred during the month, the numbers prove this narrative. By understanding the business before month end, the finance team ask the right questions and accrue for the right costs for the financial numbers. They can also write interesting commentary for the reporting packs. With startups and scaleups things move quickly, and new challenges come up all the time. Unless the finance team is kept informed and has strong relationships around the business, it can be too easy for unexpected transactions to appear, by which time it is too late.

Every corporate accountant has experienced the arrival of an unbudgeted, unexpected invoice for a project two months prior. Especially if this invoice is material, no one enjoys explaining that variance.

How partnering benefits the leadership team and the business in general

These relationships are a two-way street. Yes, the finance team benefits from the information and insight it receives, but this is only after the finance team can demonstrate its value.

All operational, sales and marketing teams have monthly, quarterly and annual goals. With fast-growing businesses, targets are often high, and the teams will need to stretch to meet these goals. Ideal for them is finance helping them achieve their goals. This help might come, for example, from identifying efficiencies and cost savings for the operational teams, enabling ROIs for the marketing teams, or providing a customer and product profitability analysis for the sales teams. The more insight the finance team can provide to help these teams achieve their goals the better. If all individuals achieve their goals, then the business should hit its goals too.

How to implement business partnerships

There are a number of steps in implementing business partnerships. Here's an overview of the main ones:

1. Deciding on the ideal business partnerships
2. Proving your worth
3. Maintaining communication
4. Sustaining your value

1. Deciding on the ideal business partnerships

If you have a larger team, you may want to delegate the 'easier' departments and take on the more difficult ones. This isn't necessarily due to personalities or how difficult a department head may be to work with; rather, the complexity of the partnership can be about how crucial the department is to business success, largely due to the goals for the year.

2. Proving your worth

Success will come down to you and your team being able to prove you're trustworthy and that you can add value. One way that trust can be earned is in providing information or completing a task to deadline and with a high-quality outcome.

Proving that you can add value is potentially the first and most important thing to consider before you even start working out who your business partners are. You can do this for all departments at once through your monthly reporting.

If your management accounts are much more than just three financial statements, are interesting to read, offer insight and have forward-looking analysis each month (see Chapter 8), the business should already know that you can add value to commercial decisions. Once you have this established, you can approach your prospective business partners and ask them how you can support them.

Important questions include:

- What information do they need?
- What do they find useful?
- What are their current sore spots? How could you support them with those?
- What are the short-term and long-term goals for their department? How can you support them to achieve these goals?

Ideally, you want the reporting that you send to other departments to be much more than the monthly accounts and departmental overhead reports. Instead, you want to be more strategic and forward-thinking. This involves providing strategic insights, forecasting future trends, and recommending actions that match with the company's and the department's strategic goals.

3. Maintaining communication

It's important to catch up regularly with each of your business partners. Start with a monthly one-to-one meeting and build up from there. If you start with understanding their department's challenges and goals, and then ensure your support meets their needs, you should find that your business partners look forward to your catch-ups and want to chat more regularly.

You may provide different metrics that can help this team decipher whether they're going to hit their goals as well as any options analysis providing useful insights for your business partners.

4. Sustaining your value

You and the finance team need to strive for continuous improvements in your support and departmental reporting. Just like with the management accounts, providing the same analysis, charts and graphs every month will create monotony and won't be interesting or useful over the longer term. Be curious about what else you can provide, dig a little deeper, and even seek feedback from the leadership team. Your relationships will then strengthen as well as provide business growth.

A seat at the table

Within this book and within my weekly blog posts, YouTube videos and FLF (Financial Leadership Fundamentals) programme, I talk about getting that 'seat at the table' as a measure of successful leadership. By this I mean that you will be invited to have a seat at the decision-making table, to be part of the team of decision makers and strategic goal makers within the business, which is largely a result of good business partner relationships. The department or leader won't make a final decision without your input.

As a new or aspiring finance leader, your goal is to get that seat at the table. It is an objective way of knowing whether your opinion is valued by the other business leaders.

If the business partner relationship isn't working, you will only be told about all the decisions (if you're lucky) when they have been made, or even worse, only when payment is due and they need this task to be completed by the finance team. In this case, you could look at the chart above in reverse:

- **Business partnership isn't working – operational.** You hear of the decisions when payment is due or a sales invoice needs to be raised.
- **Business partnership is in its infancy or needs work – information.** You hear about the decision after it has been made by the decision maker.

In contrast, if you have a seat at the table:

- **Business partnership is working – influence.** You are trusted to be part of the decision-making process, are asked for your insight and can make an impact on the decision made.

Summary

We have talked about what business partnering is, how it can benefit you, the finance function and the business, how to implement business partnering, and what I mean by gaining a seat at the table.

Actions for you:

- As part of the value-add exercise, review if business partnering can fit into the current finance structure.

- With a small finance function, you may be the business partner, so work out where you can fit this into your current workload.
- Review in your organisation who it would be best to partner with (generally leadership teams or heads of departments).
- Brainstorm ways that you could help each of these business partners and gather their operational goals (if available).
- Schedule a meeting with each leader and discuss how a business partnering relationship could work.
- Find out what their goals and objectives are and suggest ways that you can potentially help them achieve their goals.

11
Budgets, Forecasting And Growth Models

As I have discussed in earlier chapters, looking forward and strategic thinking form a big part of being a strong leader within all businesses, and especially within startups and scaleups. Budgeting and different forecasting models, including growth models, are a big part of your role. As with monthly reporting, your role as a leader is in the preparation and the communication.

Business goals before budgeting

When a budget or forecast is required, I'm often eager to jump right into the numbers and start building a model. Founders are often also keen for me to start building a budget as soon as we have started our tenure.

Before starting on that spreadsheet or opening your budgeting software, it's best to first understand the SMART (specific, measurable, attainable, relevant and timely) strategic and operational goals of the business.

There are a few reasons the goals need to be established first:

- Irrespective of how well structured the budget model is, if the budget isn't in line with the business objectives, it won't reflect what the business plans to achieve over the coming months.
- It's difficult to get buy-in from the leadership teams (and therefore from all teams) if the budget isn't based on the goals that were discussed and agreed beforehand. You are much more likely to get buy-in if you work together to achieve the same goal.
- The budget isn't there to set the goals of the business or create the vision. It should be completed beforehand by the leadership team and is created to check the financial strength of the strategic and operational goals. If the business goals don't make financial sense, they need to be changed or tweaked so that they do.

Vision, mission and strategic goals

In the life of a startup, the vision and the mission of the business are usually developed by the founders at the beginning of the business formation. This doesn't mean they can't change, but in general the founders have a mission and a vision for the business when creating the company, which is often their reason for starting a business in the first place. The vision and mission statements form the basis for determining strategic goals.

Vision and mission

A vision is what the business wants to achieve in the future or what the business aspires to become in the future. A mission statement is most often a statement on what the business does today.

A few well-known business mission and vision statements include:

- **Google's mission statement:** To organize the world's information and make it universally accessible and useful.
- **Google's vision:** To provide access to the world's information in one click.
- **Lidl's mission statement:** To offer our customers the best value for money by operating our business in a simple and sustainable way.

- **Lidl's vision:** To be the first choice for shoppers across Great Britain.
- **LinkedIn's mission statement:** To connect the world's professionals to make them more productive and successful.
- **LinkedIn's vision:** To create economic opportunity for every member of the global workforce.

Understanding the business's mission and vision helps leaders steer its priorities, goals and therefore budget in the same direction.

Strategic goals

Business strategic goals refer to a company's long-term goals. Keeping the vision in mind as well as the mission, leaders can work out what the company needs to achieve to get there. Roughly three to five strategic goals are set by a business. In general, the company may like to hit these goals over the subsequent one to three years.

Examples of strategic goals include:

- Attaining breakeven or profitability
- Increasing total revenue by a specific amount
- Increasing customer conversion rates

- Increasing customer retention by X%
- Breaking into new markets
- Building high-performing teams

Operational goals and reviews

Once a business has determined its vision and mission and its strategic goals, the leadership and management team can work out the operational goals to help the business achieve the bigger and longer-term strategic goals.

Operational goals should be set over a shorter time frame than strategic goals. Often, they are set each quarter. Businesses sometimes follow the OKRs (objectives and key results) method. Within OKRs, an objective is essentially what needs to be achieved, and the key results are the measurements of what needs to be achieved. This is a useful framework to follow to ensure that the desired result is clear.

Example of OKRs

Objective: Run the London Marathon in under 4.5 hours.

Key result 1: Finish the 'Couch to 5K' method in the next six weeks – forty minutes of non-stop running.

Key result 2: Complete the 5K to 10K training in the following eight weeks.

Key result 3: Move on to the 20K to marathon training guide for four months in the lead up to the marathon date in April 2025.

Key result 4: Do strength training one or two times per week.

With this fictional example (I hated doing my one and only half marathon and have no plans to follow this eight-month training programme!), you can see how the longer-term strategic goal might be 'Get fit and healthy'. Or it could be 'Complete bucket list before I turn fifty', which includes doing a marathon.

One operational goal to achieve these longer-term strategic goals is to run a marathon. To achieve this operational goal, there needs to be a plan in place on how to achieve it. The plan wouldn't come out of thin air, so the key results (second part of the OKRs) show what you need to achieve to hit the overall goals.

Business planning is the same. There is no point in deciding that the business wants to grow by 100% year on year if there is no idea of how the business is going to achieve this. Similarly, it's hard to build a budget if you don't know what the end goals are or what the operational and commercial teams need to do to achieve their goals.

The budget is there to check the financial validity of the strategic and operational goals. If the budget just doesn't work from a cash point of view, the leadership team needs to revisit what they want to achieve and see how they can do it more efficiently, or they need adjust the goals.

Budget communications

The first stage of planning your budget is deciding:

- Who should be involved in the budget
- What you need from them
- Your communication plan

I cannot stress enough the importance of communication when putting a budget together, particularly when involving all the leadership team. Even when I think what I have communicated is verging on overkill, someone on the leadership team will ask questions on, for example, deadlines and what is expected of them.

Because it's your job to deliver a budget, it's your responsibility to ensure that all contributors are fully aware of their role and can contribute in a timely manner. Start planning with the founder / CEO and discuss the following:

- When the budget needs to be delivered to the board (checking if there is a requirement within the shareholders' agreement).
- Who should be involved in the preparation of the budget.
- Working backwards from the board deadline, agree a timeline, starting with leadership strategy sessions or away days.
- Decide how to include who does what and when within the plan.
- Discuss and agree your communication plan.

Drivers and assumptions

Once you have the business's goals and its plans to reach these goals, you can start the budget modelling process. How to do a budget model is beyond the scope of this book. However, I do want to make a note on drivers – particularly revenue drivers – and assumptions.

One of the first steps when thinking about how to model revenue is working out what your drivers are. How does your company drive revenue or want to track revenue? What are the assumptions, and are there going to be new products and services? Take a step back and think about the answers to these questions and how else the company drives the revenue.

This topic can be discussed at length with the founders and the growth team to ensure you're all on the same page.

Whether it's driving traffic to the website and converting there, or the business has a sales team that drives the sales, or the business operates more traditionally in a physical store, starting with the end goal in mind and working backwards, how big do the drivers need to be?

Factors that need to be considered include:

- How many sales can each sales head achieve? Do you need to recruit? What is the onboarding time for each person? Are there projects to increase the volume?
- How effective are your marketing campaigns? How much traffic can they generate? What is the current conversion, and what projects are planned to improve this?
- What is the size of the market? Are there any other external factors such as competition and changes in legislation?
- Is there seasonality? Does summer, Black Friday, the Christmas period or other factors affect the business?
- What is the current level of churn? What projects are in place to improve this?

- What is the level of repeatable business or recurring revenue?
- How much volume does each customer generate?
- What is the current pricing strategy?

When considering the above, start with the assumptions and then potentially challenge the business on how to improve these things over time, ideally not all at once. For example, the commercial team may hire someone who specifically looks at churn and tries to improve the retention. After this person has been at the company for two months, the budget model could assume that churn may improve by 0.25% each month for the remainder of the year.

With all budgeting models, ensure that all the assumptions are clear, as everyone should review and confirm these assumptions. Taking the growth team as an example: work with the team to determine whether they understand the assumptions around growth and agree with them.

Generally, the assumptions within the budget model are the areas that are reviewed the most. Founders and the leadership team should review the assumptions, especially any that are within their department.

Once all the assumptions, drivers, inputs and KPIs are agreed and mapped out, it's much easier to pull together the P&L, balance sheet and cashflow.

Rolling budget

I don't know how often I've created a budget for early-stage companies, then within two months (or even less), it's out of date as the company has changed direction. I've even worked with a company that completely changed their business model within four months as they couldn't get PMF. Back to the drawing board…

For early-stage companies that are changing quickly, monthly rolling budgets and forecasts can be useful tools. The forecast is as agile as the business, and you can keep a close eye on cash runway.

While traditional budgeting provides a stable financial plan for a year, rolling budgets give you an updated twelve-month forecast every month. They also let you continuously adjust your assumptions based on the latest available data. With a brand-new business model, product or channel, every month the business is learning about what is and isn't working, and about customer behaviour. As these assumptions form the basis for revenue and for commercial funnel modelling, there is no point in keeping old assumptions that create an unrealistic P&L. This is particularly important when you are closely managing cash runway.

As the monthly cash burn can change rapidly within these smaller businesses, you need a more accurate way of forecasting runway than looking at the current month's burn. You can't do this if your budget is no longer accurate and needs to be updated. For example, if you had a conversion rate of 3% in your budget for the next month, but you had achieved only sub 2% for the last six months, the budgeted KPIs would require further adjustments and conversations with the stakeholders. Questions would include:

- How can they bridge this 1% gap, and when do we think it can be achieved?
- Is this going to affect our hiring plan?
- How is this affecting the projected cash runway?

While the business is changing rapidly, rolling budgets can be useful.

When the business is more stable, as far as the revenue and business model are concerned, rolling budgets may be more of a distraction than a useful tool. Instead of using the leadership team's (and your) time constantly reforecasting, it may be much better to spend that time improving margins and processes, growing the business, and ensuring that the targets set with the board are hit. It's a fine balance – keep this in the back of your mind.

Summary

In this chapter we have talked about business goals, including vision, mission, strategic and operational goals. Furthermore, I've covered the communications plan, assumptions of the foundation, and whether a rolling forecast is a useful tool or not.

Actions for you:

- Work with the founder to understand the business's vision, mission and strategic goals.
- Work with the leadership team to set the operational goals and understand what they are for each department as well as for the finance function.
- Ensure you're aligned with the founder/CEO regarding fundraising amounts and timing.
- Understand who to involve in the budgeting of the business. Organise a communications plan to ensure you get the input required.
- Work out the drivers and assumptions as the first step, and the budget model will be easy to build afterwards.
- Depending on the size of the company, work closely with the management teams to get their knowledge and buy-in as their targets are being set.
- Ensure the budget model is in line with the strategic and operational goals.
- If suitable to the stage of the business, implement a rolling budget.

12
Preparing To Fundraise

When working for a startup or scaleup, a big part of the finance leader's role is helping the founder run successful fundraising campaigns. I have discussed fundraising throughout this book, but there is a significant amount of preparation involved prior to a fundraise, which this chapter covers. First, though, let's go through details of an equity raise.

Different equity stages and types

Like buying a share on the stock market, investors are buying shares (generally) of the business privately, based on an agreed valuation price.

There are common stages of raising equity. This is a general overview, but all businesses could skip a stage or add additional stages in between:

1. Family and friends (and angels)
2. Seed rounds
3. Series A funding round
4. Series B, C, D, etc
5. The exit – the prize

1. Family and friends (and angels)

These investors, particularly family and friends (F&F), come in at pre-revenue stage, and founders usually go to F&F with an idea. These investments help to build the product or service and get ready for the market.

A maximum of USD2 million would be raised at this stage, but it's usually a few hundred thousand dollars to get off the ground.

2. Seed rounds

Startups can have pre-seed rounds, seed rounds, top-up and bridge rounds – all terms that are used regularly. In general, the startup has started to trade and has revenue coming in. Often it has tested for

PMF, but sometimes, particularly with pre-seed, it may need a little more funding to get there.

This is called a seed round because the founder needs funding for growth, similar to seeds growing into plants. In seed rounds founders will often approach existing investors, especially any angels, or founders will approach family offices. Family offices invest to turn a profit, but they are not representing a pool of investors such as angel groups or VCs.

Sometimes founders will find smaller VCs funding in seed rounds, but this isn't common. Often, if I do see a VC getting involved heavily in a seed round, it's because the founder is well known for a prior success.

3. Series A funding round

This is the first large round of funding. It can be anywhere between USD3 million and USD20 million dollars. More than that is rare but not unheard of.

Once a startup gets to this stage, ideally the acquisition channels are working well and efficiently, and the business knows how to grow. The founder knows that if somebody invests, for example USD1 million in sales and marketing, the return on this investment would be X in the short term and Y in the long term. The business will need to prove those marketing channels.

Some VCs or PE offices may start to be interested at this stage (in addition to existing investors), particularly the smaller VCs that are willing to take on a riskier Series A.

Finance due diligence is also becoming more common at this stage, so finance leaders would need to be prepared for that.

4. Series B, C, D, etc

I've even worked for a company that went up to Series E before an exit.

At this stage, the leadership team know the business well. The business has PMF, knows how to grow the business and has a healthy YoY growth. These rounds could be to continue with the growth trajectory by moving into new products or new markets (eg internationalisation) or investing in tech. These rounds could also facilitate an M&A event.

In general, the business needs more investment to continue with that massive growth. This is where the funding rounds can be big. If you've ever read fun headlines such as a tech business that did a raise of USD80 million or USD200 million, it's probably at this round. During these rounds, the bigger VCs and PEs become more interested, particularly the international ones or US larger VCs. The business may also attract corporate investors, particularly if a corporation sees your company as a future acquisition. They may take a small shareholding to receive the information on the company and then monitor and potentially acquire the company at a later stage. This is what happened with a company that I worked for, LoveFilm. Amazon bought a 32% stake in the company, then three years later, Amazon acquired the company.

5. The exit – the prize

This is the investors and founders' goal: to exit at a large value and cash in for millions of dollars.

The two most common events here are an IPO (initial public offering) or an acquisition. The business will need to prepare for up to two years for an IPO. At Funding Circle we did the IPO in nine months, and I can confirm that it would have been better to do it over a longer period, largely because the team would have had more time to prepare as well as shorter working days.

The business will need to decide which market to launch in. Just because the business is a UK-based company, it may not necessarily want to go on the London Stock Exchange or the AIM. It might instead want to have a US parent entity and go on the NASDAQ, for example.

Another exit is via an acquisition, where an existing corporate investor or an entirely new company will acquire all the shares of the business. Like an IPO, this can also take a long time to prepare for, and there will be a huge amount of due diligence and negotiation, particularly on price, future operations and the existing team, including the leadership team. I remember sitting in hotel rooms for a whole week with the Amazon finance team, being asked hundreds of questions during the due diligence process. It wasn't easy, but thankfully it was successful.

There are many different forms of equity. The ones I see often are:

- **Founder shares:** These are the original investments made and shares created when forming the company.
- **Share capital:** This is again about early-stage shares issued at face value.
- **Convertible loan note:** CLN is when the amount given is in the form of an option that can be converted into shares or debt. In general, the investor wants to see how the company is performing (an instrument often used at the earlier stages) and will convert to equity when satisfied or at a later round. This can be converted into debt and be repaid.
- **SAFE or ASAs:** These acronyms stand for *simple agreements for future equity* and *advanced subscription agreements*. They are other forms of

flexible agreements, which can be converted at favourable terms to the investor but are easier to execute.

- **Crowdfunding:** This is often executed by using a platform such as Indiegogo, Kickstarter, GoFundMe and Crowdcube. The amount raised is often a CLN rather than share capital.
- **Share premium:** These are shares that have been issued in later rounds and are therefore at a premium (higher valuation).

The founder's timeline

Businesses fundraise equity to start a business, to develop the products or services, or to grow the business – anything to achieve the business goals.

There are a few factors regarding the timing of fundraising and, ultimately, the exit. Have a conversation with the founder on their current thoughts (and the board's thoughts) on the timing of a potential exit.

No doubt the goal to exit will change over time, but it's a good idea to understand when they will want out of the business, as this will help you with preparing the business for the exit. Some founders want to grow their business quickly, exit and move on to the next venture. Others take a slower and more measured approach. Understanding this will change the way you plan for liquidity.

As part of those discussions, it's important to understand the estimated timelines of fundraising. What goals does the founder want to achieve before the next fundraise, and does the current cashflow forecast allow for this? Preparing for a fundraise can take many months, and you ideally want to be prepared for a fundraise with minimal effort once you have established the baseline, in particular, a good level of reporting and a working budget model.

An acquisition or an IPO can take between one and two years to complete, so the preparation is intense. Ideally, you want as much notice as possible.

How to prepare for a fundraise

A fundraise can take anywhere from three months (generally only if it's a small raise or CLN with existing investors) all the way up to eighteen months. In 2021 six months was considered a good time frame, but I'm now seeing this getting closer to nine to twelve months, and sometimes even more.

As it takes such a long time to fundraise, timing is key and there are a few important considerations, including:

1. Preparation time
2. Cash runway
3. Leadership duties
4. Communication with investors
5. Investor research

1. Preparation time

You need to ensure that the finances are sound, the KPIs are defined and collated and the unit economics make sense. You also need to prepare for the fundraise itself. This includes the pitch deck, dataroom (see below) and the storytelling: what are the numbers saying? What has the business's journey been so far, and where is it planning on going? Stories are easier to follow and are more interesting.

As there is a lot of work involved, I normally have a potential fundraise in the back of my mind at all times. If the management accounts are prepared with potential investors in mind, the balance sheet is always reconciled and clean, the KPIs are always reviewed, adjustments aren't reserved for year end, and the P&L tells the same commercial story as the business. There is then less work to do when the business decides to fundraise, and you can pivot much faster into fundraise mode.

2. Cash runway

Ideally, you want enough cash runway to last you at least as long as the fundraise process in a worst-case scenario – twelve months as well as some buffer. Ideally, I would say eighteen months. Appreciate that most startups I work with leave a lot less time than that for the fundraise process, and you must work with that decision.

3. Leadership duties

When the business starts the fundraise process, many of the company's leaders will be tied up and focused on the fundraise. It's therefore useful to have a plan for who is going to run the business when leaders – likely the founder and you – are tied up.

4. Communication with investors

With investor preparation, it's always worth the founder taking time to speak with investors. The founder should always be in fundraising mode. Potential investors can offer the founder suggestions on why they think the business is a good investment (or not). It's also easier for the founder to approach warm leads than cold leads when a fundraise process begins.

5. Investor research

Draft a list of potential investors and what each of them could offer, not just financially but also with their experience, skills and network. Consider who the business wants to be a lead investor, and who the business wants on the board.

Start with the least favourable investors and work up to the favourite. By organising it this way, the pitch will be nailed down by the time the business gets to the preferred investors.

Growth models and pitch decks

To encourage an investor to take interest in the business, the leadership team will need to collaborate to create a pitch deck and a growth model. These will both be provided to the potential investors fairly early in the fundraising process.

Growth models

Generally, a growth model is a simplified version of the internal annual budget; however, it will need to be extended to cover five years. It also clearly states the assumptions, and these are sometimes slightly more conservative for the next six months. The reason for this approach is to ensure that the business achieves the budgeted goals during the fundraising process.

Growth models also need to find that fine balance between enough growth to be exciting for an investor and growth that is so dramatic that it verges on being unreasonable and unrealistic.

Pitch decks

In 2021 all growth models looked like a hockey stick chart (a huge amount of growth that accelerated over a number of years). That sold the dream, but not all businesses can hand on heart achieve this in the current market, unless they are in a high-growth industry. Find the right balance that makes the most sense for your business.

A pitch deck is normally the first document that a potential investor will receive from the business when opening a fundraising round. The goal of the pitch deck is to tell a compelling story about the business that answers three key questions from an investor's perspective:

1. **Why should I care?** The business highlights what problem it's trying to solve, why the problem is big and why the business's unique solution helps. As a finance leader you can help the founder explain the mission and value offering clearly.
2. **Why you?** This covers the strength of the product or service, and the strength of the team

and market proposition. Here the pitch deck includes demonstrations, testimonials and even competitor comparisons.

3. **Why now?** The answer to this question explains why this is the right time for investment. Included here are the market trends, recent achievements and upcoming opportunities. Both past and future financial information would be included here as well as the pitch deck clearly stating what the funding request is – how much and what it will be used for.

As a finance leader, it's always worthwhile you going through the draft pitch deck and reviewing it as a potential investor would. Does this business look like a good investment? Do the financials align with the story? Are sections overly complex and need simplifying? Are the story and numbers consistent? Challenge the business on any of your findings to ensure that it's a strong and compelling document ready for presentation.

What turns investors off

Over the last decade, I have witnessed a few reasons for investors not being keen on investing in a business. During a fundraising round, make notes of any negative feedback, particularly if the business is in the early stage. Any repeated feedback is a brilliant takeaway for the business to work on for the next round.

Reasons can be but are not limited to the following:

- **The quality of the leadership team.** The investor would be investing and trusting the leadership team to deliver what is promised. If they can't trust what is presented, it doesn't matter how good the product is, they won't invest.
- **The investor not being convinced of growth opportunities.** This can be a combination of the product being too niche, the market opportunity being too high or the unit economics not working. The business may need to pivot or do more research.
- **No demonstration of market validation.** In this case, you need to do your homework in confirming the demand for a product or service within the target market.
- **The risks are too high.** For example, if a company in FinTech needs to be regulated and isn't yet, an investor may be concerned about the business's ability to become regulated.

What to include in the dataroom

A dataroom is a collection of documents that potential investors, VCs and lenders will have access to when they're considering investing in the company or providing debt.

I highly recommend preparing these well in advance of going to market so that you look organised and have time to prepare anything that you currently don't have. For preparing a dataroom, there are a few software options available for storing your documentation. For early stage, I tend to use Google Drive because it's free and easy. However, it's sometimes useful to pay a little for dataroom software so you have more control and it looks more professional.

I would also suggest having a subset of the dataroom – ideally one that has a minimal amount of information (like a pitch deck and basic financials) for initial discussions with investors and then all the items below for investors who are further down the discussion route and are looking more seriously at investing. This is worth discussing with your founder/CEO and deciding what is best for the business and your process.

Before going to market to fundraise, typically the following items need to be ready in the dataroom:

1. **Financial statements:** Including balance sheets, income statements and cashflow statements for the past few years. They should be easy to follow and easy to read.

2. **Forecasted business plan:** Outlining the company's goals, strategies and projections for the future. It can include information on the company's products or services, target market

and competitive landscape if these aren't already included in the pitch / commercial deck.

3. **Pitch/commercial deck:** A visual presentation that summarises the company's business plan. It is used to present the company to potential investors.
4. **Cap table:** A record of the company's equity ownership, including the names of all shareholders, the number of shares they own and the value of their shares. It should also include information about any outstanding options or warrants.
5. **Market research and industry data:** To support the business plan and financial projections. This research should demonstrate that the company's products or services have a viable market.
6. **Legal and compliance documents:** Including incorporation papers and stock option plans, and any agreements that the company has with suppliers, customers or partners. This includes contracts such as rental agreements, long-term commercial agreements, and customer terms and conditions.
7. **Intellectual property (if relevant):** Including any patents or grants, the company's IP strategy, software licence details, and domain names.

8. **Executive team's bios:** Details of the key members of the management team, including their qualifications and experience. A guideline is one or two paragraphs per team member.

9. **Bank statements:** To prove the cash total in the balance sheet.

10. **Employee information:** Being careful due to GDPR or any other data protection legislation that is relevant to you. I therefore generally provide a list of titles and start dates.

Due diligence

A due diligence is like a commercial audit. If the data-room is well prepared and the business has all the documentation ready in advance, a due diligence is straightforward, although time-consuming.

I personally have conducted small financial due diligence processes for smaller VCs and early-stage businesses. Unfortunately, around a third don't fare too well due to their balance sheets being sub-par. We have seen unreconciled bank statements that are materially out, late VAT payments that weren't declared, and cash basis financials and old control accounts that need some serious clean-ups or write-offs.

When the business has a term sheet in its hand and it loses its lead investor because the growth model or balance sheet is a mess, you may be looking for a new job. Get prepared.

Summary

We have talked about understanding the exit strategy, how to prepare for a fundraise, growth models, pitch decks, datarooms and due diligence.

Actions for you:

- Clean up your balance sheet, if you haven't already.
- Ensure your P&L makes commercial sense.
- Find out the business's exit strategy.
- Work with the founder on fundraising preparation.
- Prepare a dataroom (this can be always updated and reviewed at the point of fundraising).
- Understand what a good pitch deck looks like. You will find lots of examples online.

PART FIVE
STRATEGY

This is the fifth and final part of the Financial Leadership Fundamentals Framework. The baseline and reporting are accurate and upgraded, and you are adding value to the business. It's now time to think long term and consider the business's strategy. What does it mean to be strategic? This part focuses on developing a finance team and looking outside of the finance function, with a focus on the business model, commercial and operational challenges, particularly with a growing business.

13

Developing Your Finance Team

Perhaps you have managed one person or a team for many years and are tempted to skip this chapter. Yet leading a team is one of the most challenging and important parts of being a leader. Even if this chapter only reiterates what you have learned, it will help to refresh your mind on the importance of nurturing your team.

I have made many mistakes in the past, some of which I'll include in this chapter, and I'm still learning. My mistakes have taught me a lot, though, and this chapter will reveal how you can approach creating a strong, reliable and growing finance team that can make your life easier.

It's not all about you

When starting a career, your focus is on your own abilities, your task list and your own career. You are focused on what you're able to achieve and potentially how to please your boss.

When you start building a team, particularly as a leader, your focus pivots a little to your team's abilities, your team's roles and responsibilities, and the careers of each of your team members. You obviously need to keep learning yourself and ensuring that you achieve all the above. Particularly when working in a growing business like a startup or scaleup: if you build a team that can grow with the business and develop to be strong future leaders, you have done your job properly as a finance leader.

This not all about you, and it is also not only about getting tasks done. If you only ever talk to your team about completing their task list and then add more tasks, they aren't going to develop with the business and become a stronger team. Team development encompasses more than just the work in hand. Tasks need to get done, sure, but it can't be the focus 100% of the time.

What a finance team should look like

Perhaps you're in a role as head of finance, and you have one finance manager or one external bookkeeper.

Or you're in a finance manager role, overseeing the entire finance team. Or you're in a finance director role, and you have one analyst and one finance manager. Whatever your starting point, there should always be a plan on what the finance team could look like in two or three years' time.

I appreciate that AI may change everything, but this plan isn't stuck in stone – it's ever evolving. This plan will match where the business wants to be in two or three years' time, and it will also be worked through and communicated with the founder/CEO.

CASE STUDY: Hard work vs strategy

I remember working as a finance leader for a company that was growing rapidly – 100%, year on year. Unfortunately, my team wasn't growing, just our task list. We were one of the hardest working teams in the building and often the last to leave each day.

On occasion I would mention to the CEO that it would be useful to bring in another team member, but this was always rejected. My team and I were all heading towards burnout.

As the most senior finance team member, it was my responsibility to ensure that the team wasn't overworked and could easily manage the workload and more. But I didn't achieve this. I was too focused on the tasks in hand and short-term deadlines; I wasn't focused on developing longevity and planning for the future. Eventually, a finance leader was hired above me to sort out the finance team, who couldn't add value or be strategic. This was a huge learning experience, and I never repeated this mistake.

If you know where the finance function is heading and the founder/CEO agrees with this plan, building this team should be easier than just fighting fires and holding out too late for additional resources. As part of this plan, also identify any key person risks. Not doing so is a common problem with startups across all departments.

CASE STUDY: Lack of risk management

I once worked for a small FinTech, where we had just one person managing all the daily reconciliations – a very manual process. Being a junior, that person only had to give one month's notice. When they resigned and left the building, we hadn't found a replacement in time.

The financial controller and I had to spend way too much time reconciling while we waited for the new person to start. It wasn't pretty. I should have identified the key person risk and ensured that we had additional resources at hand, and that processes were documented and jobs shared around the team.

This illustrates why managing key person risk is so important for financial leadership and should be a significant part of strategic planning.

When to start recruiting

Looking back, I recognise that I only thought about recruiting when it was too late – when I and the team were already working too hard. If I hardly had time to complete my task list, let alone fulfilling other vital tasks such as adding value, how would I have the time to recruit a new person?

The recruitment process can take up to three months, from you and also from your team members, who will need to help with onboarding and perhaps with interviews. You'll need to work with HR too on the job description, advertising the position and interviewing candidates, which can take many hours. After onboarding a new team member, time is needed to train this person up into their new role, and it can be a month or two before they're taking over some of the task list. This whole process can be further extended if your ideal candidate has a long notice period.

If the team needs additional resources now to help with the workload, the help might come more than three months too late. Planning out a team in advance is useful. Start recruiting three months before the resources are needed, and plan ahead to ensure the team has enough resources to manage the recruitment process.

The recruiting process

Most companies have their own recruitment processes. Some companies include a five-stage process as well as a culture test and four reference checks, while other companies have shorter and simpler approaches. In general, you may not have much sway over the company's recruitment process and only be able to focus on your own part.

When I worked for Amazon, their recruitment process was intense and very lengthy. There was an HR interview, writing assessments, up to six onsite interviews and potentially further tests. It could take months, in addition to the successful candidate's notice period.

Interview tips

For startups and scaleups, if the candidate doesn't have experience in this industry, try to find out within the interview if they would be suitable. Not everyone can handle the fast pace and chaos of the finance industry.

My personal preference is to get to the know the candidate within the interview rather than grilling them with challenging questions. You can teach new skills, but you can't teach personality and culture fit. This person will be working with you and your team every working day, potentially for the next few years, and you want to ensure that they are someone that you and your team can work with.

Obviously, personality isn't everything, and I also always conduct a test. For the most junior role through to head of finance, I will do a test on Excel that involves formulas, presentation and some data analysis. I have been conducting tests like this for many years, and I am still amazed at the vast and varied answers.

Someone who is brilliant at selling themselves via an interview may fail spectacularly during the Excel test, and vice versa. The candidates who can impress you in both are the ones to hold on to.

Remember that you aren't just interviewing them – they are interviewing you too; they may not accept your offer. It is a two-way interview, and the conversations with candidates should be approached in this way. You need to sell them the role and explain what you can offer them while considering the longer-term vision for the finance team and how they fit into it.

Taking time

When you have a gap to fill (and sometimes the gap can be huge due to a recent leaver or a big new project), the instinct is to hire as soon as possible. This may work in the short term but not in the longer term. If you need a gap to be filled quickly, hire a contractor to maintain some of the work while you carry on with your recruitment process.

Take your time. Hiring isn't a race, and you need to ensure the fit is right in terms of skills, culture and future vision.

Onboarding steps

To continue showcasing my past team building mistakes, I have a great example concerning the onboarding process.

CASE STUDY: Not the right match

I onboarded a mid-level person to the team. It was for a business that was very fast growing, and my team and I were constantly firefighting. My leadership skills also weren't at their strongest at this stage of my career.

When I onboarded this mid-level person, they received about two days' worth of training with me and the team. We introduced them to all the relevant stakeholders, HR conducted their new employee process with them, and we connected them to all the relevant tech. They then received a quick overview of what they were supposed to be doing. Onboarding done.

Unsurprisingly, the person didn't pass their probationary period. They didn't know what was expected of them, and I didn't give them any feedback when I should have.

They were also surprised that they didn't pass their probationary period, which led to a difficult conversation. I still get chills thinking about it.

Looking back, this person failed due to my poor leadership, not because they weren't good enough. There aren't many juniors or mid-level new recruits who would succeed with this onboarding process.

This is another reason the timing of recruiting is essential, so you have enough time to onboard new team members properly.

Onboarding also requires a plan. I now religiously use a ninety-day plan that is communicated with the person on day one, and we have check-ins at least every two weeks to see how they are going with each milestone within the ninety-day plan. This means they know what is required of them when, they have a clear idea of who is going to help them, and anything they are struggling with can be discussed in the check-ins. By the end of the probationary period (if these still exist, pending employment law changes), this plan also means you and the new team member will know exactly whether they're good for the role or not.

Tips and challenges

One benefit of having worked with a large company that is famously good at looking after its customers but not its employees is learning what *not* to do when building a team. Along with looking after a team since 2002, I've learned a lot about what works and, of course, what doesn't work. Here are the main points that have worked for me:

- **Big picture:** Always communicate the vision, mission and strategic goals of the business so the team knows what they are working towards. The team will have their own operational goals, and it's useful to see how those fit in with the bigger picture.
- **Work–life balance:** Never text or call people outside of business hours. You're the boss, and they will feel that they must respond to messages. If you're working outside business hours, communicate via email so they can respond when they next log in. I'm often online outside business hours as I like to be flexible with the school run, etc. My team know to switch off Slack messaging notifications on their phone – I have informed them that I may Slack them out of hours, but I don't expect a response until they log in to work the following day.
- **Career pathway:** Ensure you know what each team member's career goals are and help them to achieve their goals. Whether it's about encouraging study, mentoring or additional

responsibilities in their role, as a leader, it's your job to help them get there.

- **No politics:** Writing this in 2024, my mind immediately goes to the UK and US elections, but I'm talking here about office politics within the team and the business. Encourage the team to avoid politics – it just makes working life harder and wastes time.
- **Regular feedback:** Give both positive and negative feedback swiftly (same week as the event or action, not months later), constructively (if negative) and regularly. Be aware of the recipient's emotions – you don't want to be too critical. Positive feedback isn't often remembered, whereas negative feedback is etched in, so give more positive than negative.
- **Setting a good example:** You want to be someone the more junior members of the team look up to. Stay honest, avoid politics and treat people fairly.
- **Dealing with performance issues early on:** Don't let bad performance drag on. Tackle it with encouragement to start with and try to give them the skills, education and guidance that they need to improve. If that doesn't work, you need to make a plan with HR. Failing to tackle bad performance has an adverse effect on the entire team's motivation and sometimes on culture. It can't be ignored.

Summary

This chapter has covered the structure of the finance team, recruitment, onboarding and leading a team effectively.

Actions for you:

- Think about the company's vision and goals for the next few years, and then create a team that would be able to support this business.
- Make notes of what each role could provide and what benefit it would bring to the business.
- Work out what the tipping point is for hiring this role, and plan to start the recruitment process at least three months ahead of need.
- Prepare a template onboarding plan that you can use for future hires (if HR doesn't already have one).
- Think about existing team members and work out if a ninety-day plan now could be beneficial to get them up to speed.
- If you don't already, ensure you have regular meetings with your team members to encourage feedback, career development discussions and mentoring.

14
Putting On A CFO's Hat

As a finance leader in a startup or scaleup – be that as head of finance or finance director – managing the finance function and what comes out of the department carries its own challenges. Taking that to the next level, the CFO role requires you to be much more focused on the business strategy, the industry and how to maximise the growth of the business and minimise the risks.

In general, a CFO can help with business strategy in the following ways, many of which we have covered in prior chapters:

- Financial analysis and planning
- Resource allocation
- Risk management

- Cost control
- Financial modelling
- Capital allocation
- Performance measurement
- Mergers and acquisitions
- Funding strategy
- Compliance and governance

With a startup or scaleup strategy, often the business is in its infancy and the CFO role is more hands on. This chapter gives an introduction to being a CFO for a startup or scaleup and to the main areas of focus, particularly at the early stages of a business.

Your business model

When new to a finance leadership role – via a promotion or coming in from another company – it's best to take a step back and understand the business model.

The business model is how the business creates, delivers and captures value. It's the business's value proposition, including:

- How the company is going to make revenue
- What its product or service offering is

- How it's going to deliver the product to the market

However, often companies will have multiple business models, or their model might be complicated. Sometimes the business may even need to change their business model, and as CFO you should always question this, particularly in the earliest stage or even in mid-stage. You might even be able to introduce another value proposition or tweak the current business model to avoid the need for a complete change.

CASE STUDY: New business model needed

I worked for a startup that had a marketplace business and would receive affiliate commissions based on sales.

The problem was that the sales were often completed off the platform. The process for working out the commissions and who had made a sale and who hadn't was incredibly manual, and it relied on incomplete data.

To fix this business model flaw, a subscription-based model was introduced. This meant the service providers paid a monthly fee to be included on the marketplace, and the affiliate commissions were scrapped.

This is a perfect example of challenging the business model to ensure that it works both for the business and for the consumer or, as in this case, the suppliers.

The following points give summaries of the different types of business models:

- **Subscription models:** A customer pays a recurring fee for a product or service. The business also provides ongoing value. Salesforce and Netflix are good examples.
- **E-commerce model:** A business sells products or services online. Normally, there is a digital storefront rather than a physical shop. ASOS and Amazon are two of the biggest, although most storefront retailers also have an e-commerce platform now.
- **Marketplace model:** The business works on both sides of the coin, connecting buyers to sellers. The business generally sits on a platform in the middle, earning commissions on transactions from one or both buyers and sellers. Airbnb and eBay are perfect examples.
- **Freemium model:** The business offers a basic service at no charge, normally with premium features that can be added on top. Examples are online tools or apps such as Canva and ChatGPT.
- **Pay-per-use model:** Customers are charged based on how much they use the product or service. Utilities and cloud services are examples.
- **Platform-as-a-service (PaaS) model:** A platform is provided for customers to build, deploy and

manage their own application. Examples: Oracle Cloud Platform and Microsoft Azure.

- **Direct-to-consumer (DTC) model:** Brands sell directly to consumers, not using retail. This is similar to the e-commerce model, but it can be used by a wholesaler, for example.
- **Franchise model:** An entrepreneur creates a brand that is successful, then instead of the business rolling out its own new stores, other business owners pay a licence fee to use the brand and products. This is popular within the fast-food industry, for example, McDonald's franchises.
- **Razor-and-blade model:** A product is sold at a low cost (the razor) and generates ongoing revenue for consumables (the blade). A perfect example is the printer and the ink trap, whereby a consumer buys a specific brand of printer and then has to buy ink from the manufacturer regularly.
- **Asset-light model:** The business focuses on outsourcing resources and minimising capital investments. Businesses use this model to scale quickly without buying assets. The business could white label a product or service or could use licensing, as demonstrated by Uber.

Your business may fit nicely within just one of these models, or you may have a couple or even three.

The challenge is in identifying the type of business model, so that you can leverage it. The second question is whether it is the right business model for the business. This is important, particularly at a startup. As CFO, you can work with the founder in establishing the right business model.

Once you have worked out what the business model is, you can align it with market needs. The model also determines how the business will generate revenue and its resource, technology, inventory and partnership requirements.

If you are fundraising, investors need to understand the business model so they know whether they can help your business. Certain investors prefer or have experience with certain business models.

Product–market fit (PMF)

PMF is a vital factor in deciding whether the business model makes sense or not. It is when the business decides that its product or service satisfies the need of the specific market, ie the business offering solves a real problem for a group of customers and creates enough value to make them willing to pay for it. Establishing PMF validates the business model as well as the product or service the business is providing. Establishing both the right business model and PMF is the first step in ensuring that the startup is on the right track and can now start investing in growth.

Establishing PMF

There are many ways to establish whether your business has PMF. If you want full details on how to establish a PMF, check out the book resources: www.financialleadershipfoundations.com/bookresources.

To get PMF, the business or startup may have to pivot once, twice or even three times to get there. I'm working with a business that has had to pivot three times to get PMF. Consumers like the product, but they weren't repeat buying. The business therefore had to change the product offering to ensure that consumers kept coming back.

The instances where I've found that we've had to pivot or change a business model isn't the initial sell – it's the second, third, fourth or fifth sell. It's that stickiness, that recurring revenue, that repeat custom. A CFO must always challenge the business to ensure that PMF has been met.

Commercial challenges

The illustration of a commercial funnel below summarises how all businesses market and ultimately sell their goods or services.

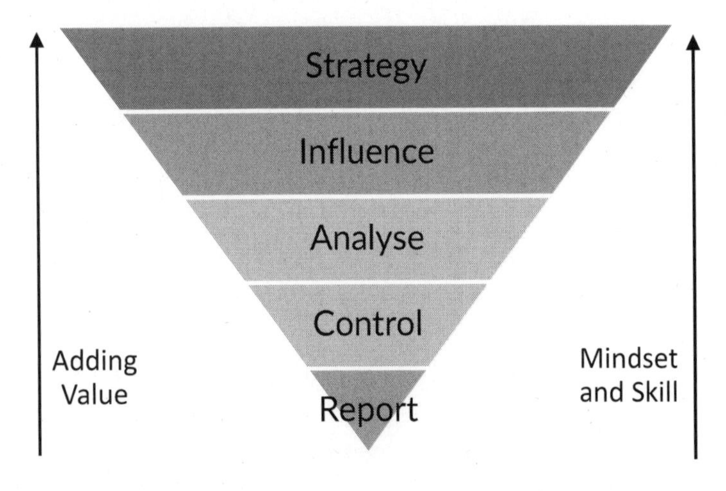

Commercial funnel

Commercial teams all focus on the process and efficiency of the commercial funnel. The funnel is relatively straightforward on the surface. First, the company wants to raise awareness, then gain market interest, find leads and then acquire them, ultimately converting a certain proportion into paying customers. After they have made the first purchase, ideally the customer will come back for repeat purchases – the business will want them to remain customers. The benefit of repeat business is no (or low) acquisition costs.

The commercial funnel therefore shows the main goals for the business, following the business determining its business model and achieving PMF. A CFO needs to have a good understanding of all stages of the commercial funnel and focus on areas where they can see significant trends (opportunities and risks), and then add insight and assistance to improve the funnel's efficiency.

Areas where a CFO can do this are:

1. **Finding customers (awareness and interest stages):**
    a. Market analysis – researching the industry and competitors
    b. Budget allocation – specifying allocation within the entire budget
    c. Cost-efficiency – working on the ROI
2. **Acquiring customers (decision and action stages):**
    a. Financial planning – determining budget allocation and ROI
    b. Performance metrics – identifying the best KPIs
    c. Capital allocation – establishing how much resources can be used
3. **Engaging customers (customer stage):**
    a. Customer retention analysis – ascertaining customer retention and whether it is enough
    b. Investment prioritisation – allocating both the ROI and resources

   c. Revenue growth – deciding if this is sufficient for hitting goals or whether there is a need to change the strategy or review the goals.

4. **Retaining customers (return and remain stages):**

   a. Churn analysis – identifying if this is at the right levels or if there is an issue

   b. Retention strategies – assessing whether they are working and if there is an ROI

   c. Customer lifetime value (LTV) and unit economics – determining if they are making sense

Before increasing marketing spend, you may find that the business isn't getting the ROI on the sales and marketing investments or costs. Challenge all stages of the commercial funnel to ensure that it is as optimal as possible. This shouldn't just be at the early stages of the business – constant review and challenge needs to continue for the entire business life cycle.

Once the company has established a solid business model, has PMF and has a solid commercial funnel with happy customers, it's time to look at growth levers. There are many different methods for growing a business, and this is where both the commercial and leadership teams can review the options. Sometimes the board is also involved in these discussions. A few areas worth considering are different products or services, channels, geographies, brand incentives and M&As.

Operational challenges

When the business is acquiring customers at a rapid rate, it's time to also focus on operations. This should ideally happen alongside the customer acquisition growth rather than afterwards.

There is a fine balance between when to increase the size of operations and the growth in customers or volume. The CFO can help with managing that balance.

CASE STUDY: Growing pains

I worked for a business that had an extreme situation with the issue of revenue growth versus operational growth.

This company was a subscription business. The demand for their product more than tripled in just a few short weeks after an event that was outside their control.

As you can imagine, their operations were not prepared for this huge increase in sales volume. It happened almost overnight, and it was an operational nightmare.

Most fast-growth businesses don't have to deal with this speed of growth and the accompanying operational challenges. It isn't uncommon, though, to hear of huge growth shutting down operations, so this does need to be closely managed.

There are five areas of operations where a CFO can help:

1. Streamlining operations
2. Resource allocation
3. Supply chain management
4. Scalability and growth
5. Risk management

As with the commercial funnel, a CFO should be looking at the overall picture. They also need to scrutinise the efficiencies and ROI on certain projects, particularly when streamlining or upgrading parts of the operations. Resource allocation is also important here due to the balancing act between investing too heavily in operations and draining resources, versus not investing enough and the operations struggling to meet increase in demand.

A CFO must monitor the operations using a combination of tools, including cashflow management, business modelling, scenario testing, and risk assessments.

Ongoing strategy and review

Particularly with startups and scaleups, you can easily spend your whole time firefighting. I schedule many blocks of time in my calendar to ensure there is space for ongoing reviews. An example is reviewing processes and quality – I regularly schedule time for these reviews in my calendar, normally once a quarter. I prefer to schedule these with the team leads at the end of the quarter and in the last week of the month.

During these reviews, I use a traffic light system to rate each area of the finance function and then of the business in red, amber or green.

With the finance function, I'm thinking about the accuracy and how automated the process is, and also how beneficial it is to the business. With financial operations, the main focus is on the accuracy and efficiency of the process, largely because any value-adding activity or analysis is reliant on the accuracy and timeliness of the data. With these processes, anything that is highlighted as red needs to be changed and should be scheduled in for a project or improvement plan.

On the business side, we're looking at the financial stability of the business, risk management, capital strategy, investor relations, compliance, any scenarios worth testing, and competition reviews.

This exercise sets up the focus for the upcoming months and quarter. A traffic light system makes it easy to do a quick review and highlight areas that need some love.

Summary

We talked about how a CFO can help with strategies including the business model, PMF, commercial challenges and operational challenges.

Actions for you:

- Take a step back. With the leadership team, work out the business model and PMF.
- Spend a lot of time ensuring that the commercial funnel is working. Look at the different elements in detail and challenge the business.
- Once the company is acquiring customers at a rapid rate, review the operations. Is it efficient? Is it scalable?
- Add a monthly review with your team leads each month.
- Add a quarterly review to go through the bigger-picture items.

Conclusion

I'm going to assume you've read this book, not just flicked through to the conclusion. That means you're now ready to go out and accelerate your finance career in the way you've been wanting to. Now you have the tools and hopefully the confidence you need to take the next step into that coveted CFO role within a startup or scaleup and be a success.

That's no small task, and I can guarantee it won't be easy. As you've read in this book, I've made countless mistakes during my finance journey so far, and I'm sure I'll make plenty more. If you keep my five-step Financial Leadership Fundamentals Framework and our book resources by your side, though, and use the strategies I've outlined, you should make a lot fewer mistakes than me.

I've walked you through what I believe from my personal experience to be the key elements of being a successful finance leader in a startup or scaleup. We've talked about the importance of making sure your baseline, your numbers and processes are robust, and that your financial reporting is accurate – the absolute essentials to being a good finance leader.

Making sure you are a great leader and that you build a strong team are also critical to your success as a CFO. Equally as important are being visible around the business and building trust with the founder/CEO and other key members from across the organisation.

We've also covered how, once you've got all these foundations rock-solid, you can move to the next level by using your finance knowledge and insight to add real value to the business and help set and achieve operational and strategic goals.

Along the way, I've pointed out that tech won't make your role redundant, and that it can help you do things better and achieve your aims. Make sure you stay on top of your finance tech, learn about what AI can do, and then use it to enhance your performance as a finance leader.

Being a great CFO in a startup or scaleup takes hard work, serious organisation and thinking outside the box. If you use my framework, though and get it right (or mostly right – we're only human, after all), it is also one of the most exciting, broad and rewarding roles you can have in your career.

What are you waiting for? Get out there and make it happen!

Next steps

My platform, www.financialleadershipfoundations.com, hosts additional resources such as downloadable templates, articles and videos, which you can access alongside this book.

If you want more information on how to implement these steps, as well as more details and group coaching sessions with me – together with the company of other new or aspiring leaders in startup and scaleups – then consider signing up to our Financial Leadership Fundamentals programme by visiting www.financialleadershipfoundations.com.

This will give you all the resources, support and knowledge required for your finance leadership career progression. All the courses are also CPD-accredited, which will cover more than a year's worth of your required CPD hours.

You'll get the support and expertise you need to wow the founder, leadership team and board with your skills, and get the promotion or positive feedback that you deserve. You'll also be able to discuss your unique position and any challenges specific to you and your business, and these problems can often be discussed and resolved in the live calls.

Glossary

AIM: Alternative investment market – a sub-market of the London Stock Exchange (LSE) for smaller- or higher-risk companies

CAC: Customer acquisition cost – how much it costs to acquire a new customer

Cap table: Capitalisation table – a list of all shareholders, how many shares they own and the percentage of ownership; also all option holders as well as the option pool

C-level: Executives of a business that have 'chief' as part of their role, for example, CEO, COO, CFO, CTO

CLN: Convertible loan note

CoS: Cost of sales

CRM: Customer relationship management – software generally used by sales and marketing for leads, prospective customers, and current and prior customers

ERP: Enterprise resource planning – software that manages and automates core processes, including finances

FP&A: Financial planning and analysis – responsibility of the commercial finance team, which generally manages the forecast and budgeting process

Fractional CFO: A CFO who works as a part-time CFO for multiple businesses

GMV: Gross merchandising value – the total value of goods or services that a business sells

GST: Gross Sales Tax

IPO: Initial public offering – the first time a private company sells shares on a public stock exchange

KPIs: Key performance indicators

LSE: London Stock Exchange

LTV: Lifetime value of a customer

M&A: Merger and acquisition

NASDAQ: National Association of Securities Dealers Automated Quotations – an American stock market

OKRs: Objective key results

P&L: Profit and loss statement

P2P: Procure to pay

PE: Private equity – PE firms buy shares in a company privately

PG: Personal guarantee (on debt)

PMF: Product–market fit

ROI: Return on investment

SaaS: Software as a service

Slack: Messaging tool (software), primarily for internal team collaboration

T&C: Terms and conditions

VAT: Value added tax

VC: Venture capitalist

WMS: Warehouse management system

References

ACCA Global, 'Finance business partner: What is a finance business partner and what do they do?' (ACCA Global, no date), https://careernavigator.accaglobal.com/gb/en/job-profiles/expert/finance-business-partner.selector.Expert.html, accessed 15 December 2024

Buckland, F, 'Feeling like an impostor? You can escape this confidence-sapping syndrome', *The Guardian* (19 September 2017), www.theguardian.com/commentisfree/2017/sep/19/fraud-impostor-syndrome-confidence-self-esteem, accessed 29 January 2025

Burke, JA and Polimeni, RS, 'The accounting profession is in crisis: A partial solution to the shortage of accountants', *The CPA Journal*

(September/October 2023), www.cpajournal.com/2023/12/01/the-accounting-profession-is-in-crisis, accessed 14 December 2024

Dunn, A, 'The Angel's in the details – make a big deal about the little things', *Medium* (29 October 2017), https://dunn.medium.com/make-a-big-deal-about-the-little-things-49044db95b3f, accessed 12 December 2024

Dweck, CS, *Mindset: How you can fulfil your potential* (Robinson, 2012)

Goleman, D, 'Leadership that gets results', *Harvard Business Review* (2000), https://content.leadershipacademy.nhs.uk/aspce3/files/Leadership_that_gets_results_goleman.pdf, accessed 13 December 2024

Google, https://about.google/intl/ALL_us, accessed 16 December 2024

Home, J, 'Imposter syndrome' (British Medical Association, 18 September 2024), www.bma.org.uk/advice-and-support/your-wellbeing/insight-and-advice/first-times-in-medicine/imposter-syndrome, accessed 16 December 2024

Kellerman, G, 'Why now, more than ever, start-ups need a good CFO', *Forbes* (17 April 2023), www.forbes.com/councils/forbesbusinesscouncil/2023/04/17/why-now-more-than-ever-start-ups-need-a-good-cfo, accessed 14 December 2024

Kirk, I, 'How many Britons display signs of impostor syndrome?' (YouGov, 7 June 2022), https://yougov.co.uk/society/articles/42482-how-many-britons-display-signs-impostor-syndrome, accessed 13 December 2024

KPMG, *Mind the Gap* (KPMG, 2022), https://assets.kpmg.com/content/dam/kpmg/xx/pdf/2022/12/mind-the-gap.pdf, accessed 13 December 2024

Lidl, https://careers.lidl.co.uk/life-at-lidl/about-lidl#our-vision-mission, accessed 16 December 2024

LinkedIn, https://about.linkedin.com, accessed 16 December 2024

May, R, 'Start-ups across the UK are going bust – they need more careful management for our economy to boom', *The Telegraph* (24 January 2019), www.telegraph.co.uk/politics/2019/01/24/start-ups-across-uk-going-bust-need-careful-management-economy, accessed 14 December 2024

Rani, P, 'Eight ways to be a better leader', *Times Higher Education* (29 March 2024), www.timeshighereducation.com/campus/eight-ways-be-better-leader, accessed 9 December 2024

Watkins, MD, *The First 90 Days, Updated and Expanded: Proven strategies for getting up to speed faster and smarter* (Harvard Business Review Press, 2013)

World Economic Forum, *Future of Jobs Report 2020* (WEF, October 2020), www3.weforum.org/docs/WEF_Future_of_Jobs_2020.pdf, accessed 14 December 2024

Acknowledgements

I'd like to thank all the founders, finance teams and students I have worked with through my corporate career and through Fast Growth Consulting and FLF programme. I have learned so much and grown so much as a result.

I want to thank the CFOs I have worked for over the years: Kim Peak and Meredith Hilsberg in Australia, Jim Buckle and Sean Glithero in the UK. Many of their teachings are included in this book, and I wouldn't be where I am today if it wasn't for them.

I want to thank my beta readers, for the invaluable feedback and time they dedicated to make this book much better than the first draft. Thanks too to Jim Buckle, who also volunteered time to put together the foreword; Lucy Wood, who is always supportive and amazing; Lukasz Wiertel, who has been part of both the LoveFilm and Funding Circle journey, so he knows; Christi Warren, who graciously gave up her time; and Mum, who loves a grammar challenge, being the brilliant teacher she is. Everyone here gave up their time for me, was super-supportive, and I can't thank these people enough.

I want to thank my team at Fast Growth – Sadaf, Christi and Grace. I really enjoy working with you, and FGC wouldn't be where it is without your patience, dedication and help.

Finally, thanks to my supportive husband, children and family for encouraging me to write this book.

The Author

Alysha Randall completed a Bachelor of Commerce at La Trobe University in Melbourne and became a qualified CPA before moving to London in 2006. Here she was introduced to the world of startups and scaleups. Starting at LoveFilm in 2006, she took on the role of director of finance, and she worked for Amazon as they acquired the business. Alysha then moved over to Funding Circle and, after building a finance team, worked on its exit to LSE. In 2019, Alysha founded Fast Growth Consulting Ltd. She has since collaborated with multiple fast-growth businesses, such as Collagerie, GoTrade, Just Move In, Legl, SideQuest VR, Super Payments and VenueScanner. She conducts courses to train new and aspirational FDs and CFOs. In 2021 she became a treasurer trustee for the charity Sustainable Merton.

Alysha lives in London with her husband and two children and can do all this thanks to copious amounts of coffee.

www.financialleadershipfoundations.com

www.linkedin.com/in/alysharandall

www.youtube.com/@FinancialLeadershipFoundations